THIS BOOK BELONGS TO:

....

CHRISTMAS 2007

Christmas
with Southern Living
2007

Christmas
with Southern Living
2007

Oxmoor
HOUSE®

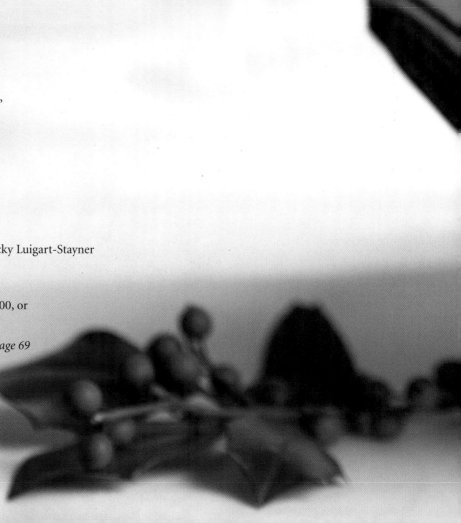

©2007 by Oxmoor House, Inc.
Book Division of Southern Progress Corporation
P. O. Box 2262, Birmingham, Alabama 35201-2262

ISBN-13: 978-0-8487-3152-6
ISBN-10: 0-8487-3152-2
ISSN: 0747-7791
Printed in the United States of America
First Printing 2007

Editor in Chief: Nancy Fitzpatrick Wyatt
Executive Editor: Susan Carlisle Payne
Managing Editor: Allison Long Lowery

Christmas with Southern Living® 2007
Editor: Rebecca Brennan
Foods Editor: Julie Gunter
Senior Copy Editor: L. Amanda Owens
Copy Editor: Donna Baldone
Editorial Assistant: Rachel Quinlivan, R.D.
Senior Designer: Melissa Jones Clark
Photography Director: Jim Bathie
Senior Photo Stylist: Kay E. Clarke
Associate Photo Stylist: Katherine Eckert
Test Kitchens Director: Elizabeth Tyler Austin
Test Kitchens Assistant Director: Julie Christopher
Food Stylist: Kelley Self Wilton
Test Kitchens Professionals: Kathleen Royal Phillips,
  Catherine Crowell Steele, Ashley T. Strickland
Director of Production: Laura Lockhart
Senior Production Manager: Greg A. Amason
Production Assistant: Faye Porter Bonner

Contributors
Indexer: Mary Ann Laurens
Writers: Amy Edgerton, Amelia Heying
Editorial Assistant: Laura K. Womble
Photographers: Beau Gustafson, Lee Harrelson, Becky Luigart-Stayner
Photo Stylists: Melanie J. Clarke, Kappi Hamilton
Test Kitchens Professional: Jane Chambliss

To order additional publications, call 1-800-765-6400, or
  visit **oxmoorhouse.com.**

Cover: Cheesecake-Stuffed Dark Chocolate Cake, *page 69*

Back cover: *(clockwise from top left)*
  Cran-Ginger Granita, *page 138;*
  Clearly Charming, *pages 40–41;*
  Turkey and Black Bean Chili, *page 64;*
  Tradition with a Twist, *page 111*

Contents

Decorating

Cooking & Baking

Entertaining

Giving

Holiday Planner . . . 177

Decorating

Oh what fun it is to array every room in the house
with holiday trimmings! These pages will inspire you with
delightful accents and innovative arrangements to deck
your home with Yuletide cheer.

Front Door Greetings

Welcome the holidays—beginning with your front door.
Take a look at these trimmings that give traditional embellishments
a fresh twist. Then copy the ideas presented here, or use them as
the starting point for your own imaginative decorations.

Elegance Squared

These simple wreaths use inexpensive picture frames as their base. To make a wreath, attach sprigs of evergreen—such as cedar, pine, or cypress—to the frame with florist wire. Crisscross ribbons along the wreath, securing the ends with wire. Insert florist picks with wire into fruits, and then wire them to the wreath. To connect two wreaths, wire the bottom wreath to the top and cover the wire with ribbon. Then wire a bow to the top of the wreath. After the holidays, remove the fruits and greenery, and store the picture frames until next season.

Big on Style

Frame the front door with giant packages for easy, inexpensive impact. (Check out ribbon and wrapping paper at discount and "dollar" stores.) For each grouping, put a brick or other heavy object in the bottom box to anchor the display. Then wrap the cardboard boxes with brightly colored papers, stack them, and tie them with a big bow. Be sure to place the boxes under a covered entry.

A Fine Finish

Glue red reindeer moss to a cluster of inexpensive plastic bells for a chic door enhancement. Wire or tie a big bow at the top of the bells. (We found these bells for under $10 at a discount store. Look for reindeer moss at discount and crafts stores.)

Mantels
for Many
Moods

Plan your holiday mantel to complement
the colors and ambience of your room. The
decorations on these pages show a range of
styles suitable for a variety of settings—all
are equally festive.

Serene Scene

A neutral-toned backdrop gets a warm holiday glow from a simple arrangement of pillar candles and bud vases filled with bittersweet branches. For visual interest, mix pillars of varying heights and hues and set them on small boxes or books to add height where needed. Arrange the candles and vases of bittersweet before Thanksgiving for an autumn decoration, and then all that's needed is an evergreen garland to take the decoration through the Christmas season.

Red-hot Style

Make a bold statement with vivid red. Fill containers with bright amaryllis blooms, pepper plants, and bunches of berries. Use red containers to give an additional pop of color. Then tuck pine clippings and pinecones around the bases of the containers. For guaranteed holiday sparkle, punctuate the look with votive candles.

Grand Scale

An ornate fireplace needs only a few embellishments to set the holiday mood. For a room with high ceilings and a large mantel, opt for tall decorations, such as these silver twig trees that grace each end of the ledge. A glittery star garland and silver ornaments echo the metallic theme. Fill in with smaller items, such as these clear vases holding tiny nosegays of freesia and berries. Add a fun detail to the arrangements by knotting a narrow leaf around each bunch of flower stems (see detail at right). Then place pillar candles along the mantel for a cheery glow, and soften the arrangement with clippings of evergreen.

Refined Approach

To create a floral extravaganza, start by protecting the mantel ledge with plastic (use a large trash bag or other waterproof covering). Arrange water-soaked blocks of florist foam on top of the plastic. (For best results, use florist-foam blocks in cages or on trays to help prevent water damage.) Now, for the fun part! Assemble your choice of flowers, dried materials, and fruits. Insert the stems into the florist foam; use florist picks to add fruits to the arrangement.

For a design that transcends the seasons, gather an assortment of dried materials, seedpods, and pinecones (no need to soak the florist foam for dried materials). At Christmastime, swap the dried materials or just fill in around them with fresh flowers and fruits. For a special party, layer on lushness with grapefruit and pomegranate halves secured with florist picks. To balance the arrangement, place clear urns filled with pinecones, nuts, fruits, ornaments, and feathers at the ends of the mantel.

▲ Staying Power

Go easy on your holiday flower budget by glorifying inexpensive blooms, such as carnations. To achieve the look pictured here, place a water-soaked florist-foam sphere in a decorative container and insert carnation stems to completely cover all visible areas of the foam. The moistened foam will keep the blooms fresh for several days.

Cheerful Expression ▶

Red and green set an instant holiday scene. Hang richly colored stockings for the ultimate declaration of traditional style; then add a snow white stocking to the mix to make the colors really pop. For the mantel, create a display from favorite accessories. Here, metal letters on stands take center stage, with flower-filled pots, crimson candles, and a fragrant wreath playing supporting roles. Use books and boxes to vary the heights of the individual elements.

A Cowboy *Christmas*

Rustle up some fun with Western-inspired holiday accessories.
Establish the theme with a few key items, and then add such embellishments
as lariat wreaths, bandanna napkins, rustic metal accents, and
lots of greenery and pinecones.

All Spruced Up

Corral a tree full of cowboy ornaments to celebrate the Western-style scheme. Or purchase several trimmings with a cowboy motif, place them in prominent places on the tree, and then fill in with solid-colored ball ornaments and metal stars. Drape a rope along the branches as a garland, and perch a cowboy hat on the uppermost branches as a tree topper.

Westward Ho! Ho! Ho!

These boots aren't made for walking, but they sure dress up a mantel. Center a trio of boot vases filled with holly berries, and hang cowboy boot stockings to kick up the charm. Place tall pieces, such as candleholders (left), at the ends of the mantel to frame the arrangement. Then scatter smaller items, such as votive candles and pinecones, to add interesting color and texture. Attach a Western-look garland or ornaments to an evergreen garland, and finish with a rope "wreath" befitting the cowboy theme.

▲ Name Your Pardner

Set ornaments alongside place settings for a clever way to use small boot ornaments somewhere other than the tree. Then write guests' names on small cards stamped with a Western-themed decoration; tuck a card and a sprig of rosemary or greenery into the top of each boot.

◀ Dinnertime Roundup

This table offers more refined seating than gathering around the campfire, but the rustic appeal is indisputable. Use a Navajo blanket as a table runner, and fill boot vases with stems of holly berries. Set places with pottery dishes in turquoise, deep red, and brown; then accent with antler flatware and bandanna-style napkins.

A Spot *of* Cheer

Tabletop arrangements add sparks of holiday
spirit to any room in your home. These ideas work well on
sideboards and foyer tables, but consider adapting
them for the mantel as well.

◄ Gallery Under Glass

Want a new way to show off favorite holiday photos? Glue snapshots to decorative papers, and trim the edges for a framed effect. Prop the photos on plates or footed stands, and cover with glass cloches. Surround the photos with angel hair and frosty ornaments for a wintry look.

▲ Now Showing

Display Christmas cards like miniature works of art on small plate stands (or on a hand-towel stand as shown at right) to enjoy throughout the season. Scatter glittery ornaments, ribbons, and candies among the cards to embellish the grouping.

Pretty Special ▶

Believe it or not, this exquisite topiary is easy to make. Fill a container with plastic craft foam. Hide the foam by covering it with reindeer moss, and insert a wooden dowel into the foam. Soak a florist-foam sphere in water, and then let it drain; press the sphere onto the top of the dowel until it feels secure. Cover the sphere entirely with reindeer moss, using U-shaped florist pins. Insert blooms into the sphere, as desired. Wrap the dowel with ribbon, and tie a bow at the base of the flower-covered sphere. Vary the size and height of this design to suit your space.

▼ All Is Bright

Nothing adds sparkle to a holiday display quite like candlelight. Tall tapers in a complementary shade of green twinkle beside a Santa duet, while white votives in clear holders cast a cheery glow.

A Glorious Gathering

A tabletop grouping showcases treasured Christmas collectibles for all to enjoy.
Choose items that share similar colors or themes, and heighten the festive ambience
by adding ribbons and ornaments to the arrangement.

Visions of Candy Canes

Red and white stripes—whether on luscious lollipops or towering amaryllis—are signs of the season. Check out the photos on these pages for innovative ways to dress your home with this cheery color combination.

All Set for St. Nick

For a twist on tradition, substitute upside-down Santa hats for standard stockings. Adorn the rest of the mantel with a cheery mix of snowmen, potted paperwhites, and striped sweets. For a windowlike focal point, lean a mirror against the wall and hang a wreath from the top. Complement the red-and-white scheme with touches of soft blue, such as with the blue pots and wrappings shown here.

Let It Snow

A winter wonderland of marshmallow snowballs and whimsical snowmen creates a scenic setting for the holiday's traditional treat: peppermint candy. Accent with blue glassware, napkin trims, and lollipops for fresh counterparts to the red-and-white hues. Use personalized place cards, such as these picture frame ornaments, to guide guests to their places at the table.

Candy Land

Set a jolly mood with a sweet centerpiece. Use purchased boxes or decorate your own with red and white dots and stripes. (Look for boxes at discount and crafts stores.) Fill a small box halfway with plastic craft foam, and place it on top of a larger box. Insert candy canes and lollipops into the foam. Cover the top of the foam with miniature and jumbo marshmallows; sprinkle more on the tabletop to simulate mounds of snow. Dot the scene with snowmen and other holiday decorations.

Red-and-White Delight

Candy cane tapers set aglow a glorious creation of rosebuds, hypericum berries, and evergreen sprigs. To make the arrangement, place a block of moistened florist foam on a cake stand. Insert the striped candles securely into the top of the foam, making sure they don't tilt. Clip the flower stems, leaving 1 to 2 inches of stem beneath each bloom. Insert the stems into the sides of the foam. Fill in around the flowers and candles with berries and greenery to completely cover the foam.

To keep the flowers fresh for several days, carefully add water to the florist foam every day or so. As the flowers fade, replace them with pinecones or additional greenery and berries. The greenery and berries will stay fresh for at least a week.

Fresh Take

Here's a new way to use amaryllis, one of the season's most distinctive plants: Fill a casserole dish or container of your choice with wheatgrass. Clip the amaryllis, leaving their stems long. Insert a long florist pick into each stem, and then stick the flowers into the bed of grass. (You can find wheatgrass at health-food stores or farmers' markets; or see our directions for growing ryegrass on page 114.) This happy pairing is equally at home on a kitchen counter or mantelpiece.

Clearly *Charming*

Gather your favorite glass containers, and you'll be well on your way to fresh, fun holiday accents for your home. These pages show seven simple ideas. Once you get started, you're sure to come up with dozens more!

Group Dynamic

Arrange several clear vases together to make a striking display. Fill the containers with colorful fruits, nuts, and candies. Try tying together floral nosegays and placing them in water-filled vases (above). Or wrap the stems with leaves, and pin in place with boutonniere pins (below). To hold flowers underwater, gently place one or two clear glass marbles inside each bloom. Use a place mat underneath the containers to unify the grouping.

Tall and Elegant

See that your display garners great attention by stacking cake stands to increase the height. Use bud vases to hold a monochromatic array of stems, and reinforce the scheme by laying down a length of fabric, tablecloth, or napkin in the same color. Place the setup in front of a mirror to increase the impact.

Simple Style

What could be easier and lovelier than stacked cake stands accented with seasonal fruits? To play up the festive mood, tuck in sprigs of holly. For a special party or dinner, add winter white freesia blooms.

Just Add Water

Use a wide glass container, such as a punch bowl, to house a dramatic floral arrangement. Fill the bowl about a quarter full with water. Cut the stems of large flowers, such as amaryllis, a couple of inches below the blooms, and float them on top of the water. Finish by inserting lacy evergreen clippings among the blooms. Float candles around the outside of the arrangement, keeping the flames well away from the plants.

Oh So Bright

To cast a merry glow, securely fit several taper candles into a clear glass vase. Then add a brightly colored ribbon for a festive touch.

Center of Attention

A pair of glass vases filled with ornaments and topped with gazing balls make a radiant centerpiece. To make the ring of flowers and berries to encircle a gazing ball, place a small moistened florist-foam wreath on the rim of a vase (left). Clip the flower stems 1 to 2 inches beneath the blooms, and then push the stems into the foam to cover. Place a gazing ball on top of the foam; tuck in berries, as desired. Scatter ornaments and greenery clippings around the arrangement.

Sparkle and Shine
When there's no room on your tree for even one more ornament, place the extras in clear containers for a quick and easy decoration. Fill in around the baubles with beaded and sequined garlands. Display the vases on a sideboard or mantel for a shimmery accent.

Holiday Bowl

With this clever decoration, a colorful transition from Thanksgiving to Christmas can be just as natural inside as it is out.

Basic Construction

Choose a wide, sturdy decorative bowl. Gather candles of varying widths, heights, and shades. For an autumn look, select candles in rust, orange, and golden hues; or consider using white or cream ones that transcend the seasons. If necessary, securely elevate the candles on a base in the bowl to add height and to raise the flames above nearby foliage. Once you're happy with the candle arrangement, fill the bowl with dried leaves and berries, tucking in stems randomly around the candles. Scatter small gourds and pumpkins around the bowl.

Christmastime Is Here

After Thanksgiving, substitute materials in the bowl to create a Yuletide array.
Replace autumn-colored candles with pillars in shades of green. Remove the dried
leaves, and tuck in an assortment of evergreen sprigs and berries. Complete the look
by surrounding the bowl with tiny wrapped boxes and bright green apples.

White Christmas

Even in the South, where temperatures can be downright balmy
in December, you can infuse your interiors with a refreshing hint of
snow. Look for inspiration in these all-white decorations.

Marvelous Monotones

Explore the spectrum of neutral colors—from khaki and beige to ivory and pearl—for a single-hued palette that allows for a variety of shapes and sizes that won't compete for attention. Combining green plants with pitchers, pots, and other ceramics brings new life to everyday treasures in a fresh yet traditional mantel setting.

The Height of Ornamentation

Because a chandelier commands attention regardless of the season, it's the perfect piece for introducing holiday ambience. Dangle white ornaments from dainty ribbons for a fun, frosty outlook. Punch up the glamour with loops of shimmery garlands, and sprinkle abundantly with snowflakes in a mix of shapes and sizes.

◀ Smart Additions

On its own, a single pillar candle may lack pizzazz, but elevating it on a cake stand takes it to a new level. To up the charm quotient, encircle the candle with interesting accents, such as the metal reindeer pictured or a favorite collection of elf or Santa figurines. Layer wispy branches of cedar or cypress around the base of the cake stand, and add a dusting of faux snow to unify the look.

▼ Fresh Focus

Chunky pillar candles rising from a circlet of carnations create a centerpiece with staying power. To ensure several days of fresh blooms, start with a moistened florist-foam wreath. Place the wreath form on a tray to protect the tabletop from moisture. Clip the carnation stems about 1 to 2 inches below the blooms; stick the stems into the wreath, completely covering the top and sides. Place the candles in the center of the wreath. Accent with small fruits (such as Seckel pears and kumquats), graceful loops of ribbon, and votive candles in clear holders.

Little Trees with Big Appeal

Spread Christmas cheer to every room in your home. You need only a small area to showcase these diminutive delights.

Monkeying Around

Give little ones their own tree—and encourage them to trim it with favorite toys, such as the sock monkeys pictured here—to get children involved in the holiday decorating. Place an artificial tree (needs no water!) in a wagon to provide a stable base. Tuck cedar, cypress, or pine clippings among the branches for an enchanting evergreen scent, as well as a more natural appearance. Fill the wagon with wrapped packages to hide the base of the tree—and to build the excitement for little ones.

Countdown to Christmas

Heighten anticipation with an Advent tree dotted with numbered cookies. (To keep the cookies fresh, place them in small cellophane bags tied at the top with ribbon.) As a cookie is taken from the tree each day, replace it with an ornament to keep the tree fully decorated right up to Christmas Day. Place the tree in front of a mirror to double the sparkle effect.

Branch Out

Arching branches clipped from your yard form an elegant tree that can be used indoors or out. Fill a heavy container with plastic craft foam, and stick the branches into the foam. Cover the top of the foam with moss, gluing or pinning it in place. Use long loops of ribbon to dangle glistening ornaments from the branches.

▲ A Show of Favorites

Build your own unconventional tree by using stacked cake stands as the landscape for a high-rise Christmas village that showcases your special small-scale holiday collectibles. Blanket the display with a scattering of faux snow.

◀ Create a Scene

Fashion a festive vignette by trimming a small potted evergreen in an earthenware crock with country-look ornaments and a braided-straw star topper. Pull out everyday items from the kitchen—such as metal canisters, egg crates, and rooster figurines—to make a lighthearted display.

Cooking & Baking

Featured on these pages are our most impressive
make-ahead party foods, 30 minutes-or-less fare for
the busy holiday host, kids in the kitchen fun, and
our best-ever brownies and cookies.

Christmas *Express*

Check out this easy and fast holiday fare—each recipe is
ready in 30 minutes or less and many can be made ahead.

Spicy Crawfish Spread

Serve this sassy Cajun spread with corn chips, vegetable crudites, or crackers.

Prep: 4 min. Cook: 6 min.

3	Tbsp. butter
¾	cup finely diced onion
¾	cup finely diced celery
4	garlic cloves, minced
2	Tbsp. all-purpose salt-free seasoning blend (we tested with Paul Prudhomme's Magic Seasoning)
½	tsp. cayenne pepper
8	oz. peeled, cooked crawfish tails, finely chopped
1	(8-oz.) package cream cheese, softened

Garnish: celery leaf

Melt butter in a small skillet over medium-high heat. Add onion, celery, and garlic; sauté 5 minutes or until onion and celery are tender. Add seasoning blend and pepper; sauté 30 seconds. Combine sautéed vegetables and crawfish tails in a bowl. Add softened cream cheese, and stir gently to combine. Garnish, if desired. **Yield: 2¼ cups.**

Spicy Crawfish Spread

Orecchiette with Broccoli in Garlic Oil

This simple pasta dish offers a nice way to get kids to eat broccoli.

Prep: 4 min. Cook: 22 min.

1	Tbsp. salt
1	(12-oz.) package orecchiette pasta (about 4 cups) or other small shaped pasta
1	(12-oz.) package fresh broccoli florets
½	cup olive oil
8	garlic cloves, thinly sliced
¾	tsp. salt
¼	tsp. dried crushed red pepper
3	Tbsp. minced fresh flat-leaf parsley

Stir 1 Tbsp. salt and pasta into 3 qt. boiling water in a Dutch oven. Cook 3 minutes less than package directions state. Stir in broccoli florets; cook 3 minutes or until pasta is al dente, and broccoli is crisp-tender. Drain and return pasta and broccoli to Dutch oven.

While pasta cooks, combine olive oil and next 3 ingredients in a small saucepan. Cook over medium-low heat 6 minutes or until garlic is golden, stirring often. Remove from heat. Add garlic oil and parsley to pasta, and toss well. Serve hot. **Yield: 4 servings.**

Raspberry-Glazed Beets with Chèvre

Goat cheese makes a wonderful finishing touch for these slightly sweet, quick-to-heat beets.

Prep: 2 min. Cook: 15 min.

¾	cup chicken broth
½	cup red raspberry preserves (we tested with Smucker's Simply Fruit)
¼	tsp. salt
3	(14½-oz.) cans sliced beets, drained
¼	cup butter or margarine
¼	cup crumbled chèvre

Bring first 3 ingredients to a boil in a large saucepan over high heat. Add beets, and boil 8 to 10 minutes or until liquid is reduced to a syrup, stirring often. Remove from heat. Stir in butter. Top each serving with crumbled chèvre. Serve immediately. **Yield: 8 servings.**

Stovetop Sweet Potatoes with Maple and Crème Fraîche

These sweet potatoes are beaten with a mixer and heated on the stove, keeping your oven free for other holiday baking. Crème fraîche is a surprise ingredient blended in along with maple syrup for an indulgent twist to traditional sweet potato casserole. And instead of marshmallow topping, try these cinnamon-glazed pecans. You won't be able to stop nibbling on them.

Prep: 8 min.   Cook: 15 min.

2	cinnamon sticks, broken
¼	cup sugar
3	Tbsp. butter
1	cup pecan halves
¼	tsp. salt
3	(15-oz.) cans candied yams or sweet potatoes in syrup, drained
¼	cup butter, softened
2	Tbsp. finely chopped crystallized ginger
1	tsp. salt
¼	tsp. freshly grated nutmeg
1	cup crème fraîche*
¼	cup pure maple syrup
1	tsp. maple extract or vanilla extract
1	tsp. balsamic vinegar

Grind cinnamon sticks to a fine powder in a coffee grinder; set aside.

Cook sugar and 3 Tbsp. butter in a small saucepan over medium-high heat 3 minutes or until melted and golden. Add pecans, and cook 2 minutes until pecans are toasted and glazed, stirring frequently.

Stir in cinnamon and ¼ tsp. salt. Spread pecans on wax paper, and set aside to cool.

Combine sweet potatoes, ¼ cup butter, ginger, 1 tsp. salt, and nutmeg in a large bowl. Beat at low speed with a hand mixer 1 minute; beat at high speed 2 minutes.

Gently fold crème fraîche, maple syrup, extract, and balsamic vinegar into sweet potatoes. Transfer to a saucepan. Bring to a simmer over medium-low heat. Simmer, covered, 10 minutes, stirring occasionally. Spoon potatoes into a serving dish, and sprinkle with glazed pecans. **Yield: 8 to 10 servings.**

*Find crème fraîche with other specialty cheeses in the deli section of many upscale markets.

Roasted Broccoli with Orange-Chipotle Butter

Here's a high-flavored side dish worthy of the finest dinner menu. Fresh orange flavor and smoky chipotle pepper hit hot roasted broccoli and sizzle with goodness. Chicken, beef, or pork make fine partners.

Prep: 2 min.   Cook: 17 min.

2	(12-oz.) packages fresh broccoli florets
2	Tbsp. olive oil
¼	cup butter, softened
2	tsp. freshly grated orange rind
1	tsp. minced canned chipotle peppers in adobo sauce
½	tsp. salt

Combine broccoli and oil in a large bowl; toss to coat. Place broccoli in a single layer on an ungreased jelly-roll pan. Roast at 450° for 15 to 17 minutes or until broccoli is crisp-tender.

While broccoli roasts, combine butter and next 3 ingredients in a large bowl. Add roasted broccoli to bowl, and toss to coat. Serve hot. **Yield: 6 to 8 servings.**

Roasted Broccoli with Orange-Chipotle Butter

Crisp Chicken with
Hearts of Palm Salad

quick & easy

Crisp Chicken with Hearts of Palm Salad

Prep: 17 min.   Cook: 9 min.

4   skinned and boned chicken breasts (about 1½ lb.)
1   cup Japanese breadcrumbs (panko)
1   large egg
½   tsp. salt
½   tsp. freshly ground black pepper, divided
5   Tbsp. olive oil, divided
1   (14-oz.) can hearts of palm, drained and sliced
½   cup diced red onion
1   small green bell pepper, diced
1   Tbsp. red wine vinegar
2   Tbsp. chopped fresh flat-leaf parsley or cilantro
Garnish: flat-leaf parsley or cilantro

Place chicken between 2 sheets of heavy-duty plastic wrap; flatten to ¼" thickness using a meat mallet or rolling pin. Spread breadcrumbs in a shallow plate. Beat egg in a shallow bowl.

Sprinkle chicken with salt and ¼ tsp. pepper. Dip 1 chicken breast in beaten egg; coat with breadcrumbs. Repeat with remaining chicken. Cook chicken in ¼ cup hot oil in a large skillet over medium-high heat 4 minutes on each side or until done.

While chicken cooks, make salad. Gently toss together remaining 1 tablespoon oil, remaining ¼ tsp. pepper, hearts of palm, and next 4 ingredients. Serve chicken topped with salad. Garnish, if desired. **Yield: 4 servings.**

Turkey and Black Bean Chili

Heat oil in a Dutch oven over medium-high heat. Add turkey and salt; cook, stirring until turkey crumbles and is no longer pink. Push meat to outer edges of pan, and add onion and garlic to center of pan. Sauté 3 minutes.

Add chili seasoning, and cook 1 minute. Add tomatoes, broth, chipotle pepper, and 1 Tbsp. adobo sauce. Bring to a boil. Cover, reduce heat, and simmer 5 minutes. Add beans; cook 5 minutes or until thoroughly heated. Serve with desired toppings. **Yield: 6 cups.**

quick & easy

Broiled Sirloin with Smoky Bacon Mushrooms

Using precooked bacon and presliced mushrooms gets this gourmet fare to the table fast.

Prep: 8 min.   Cook: 16 min.   Other: 5 min.

4	fully cooked hickory smoked bacon slices
1	medium onion, cut vertically into thin slices
1	Tbsp. butter, melted
2	garlic cloves, minced
2	(8-oz.) packages sliced fresh mushrooms
1¾	tsp. salt, divided
3	Tbsp. chopped fresh flat-leaf parsley
⅛	tsp. freshly ground black pepper
2	(1-lb.) sirloin steaks (1¼" thick)
½	tsp. freshly ground black pepper

Reheat bacon according to package directions until crisp; coarsely crumble. Sauté onion in butter in a large skillet over medium heat 5 minutes until beginning to brown. Stir in garlic, mushrooms, and ¾ tsp. salt. Sauté 10 minutes or until mushrooms are tender and liquid evaporates. Stir in bacon, parsley, and ⅛ tsp. pepper.

While mushrooms cook, sprinkle both sides of steaks with remaining 1 tsp. salt and ½ tsp. pepper.

Broil 5½" from heat 7 minutes on each side or until desired degree of doneness. Let stand 5 minutes before slicing. Cut steaks into thin slices; arrange on a serving platter, and top with mushrooms. **Yield: 4 to 6 servings.**

make ahead • quick & easy

Turkey and Black Bean Chili

Take advantage of packaged seasoning mixes, such as the chili mix called for below. Seasoning mixes are great because they include a number of spices in one package so they cut down on the time it takes to measure individual spices. We used canned black beans here but pinto or kidney beans are equally good.

Prep: 5 min.   Cook: 19 min.

2	Tbsp. olive oil
1¼	lb. ground turkey
½	tsp. salt
1	large onion, chopped
2	Tbsp. chopped garlic
1	(1.25-oz.) package chili seasoning mix
1	(15-oz.) can diced tomatoes in sauce or crushed tomatoes in puree
1	cup chicken broth
1	chipotle pepper in adobo sauce, chopped
1	Tbsp. adobo sauce
1	(15-oz.) can black beans, rinsed and drained

Toppings: sour cream, shredded Monterey Jack cheese, fresh cilantro sprigs, diced avocado

Pepper Steak with Roasted Red Pepper Pesto

Using a grill pan allows you to grill year-round. A cast-iron skillet works well as a grill pan substitute.

Prep: 4 min.   Cook: 15 min.

1½ lb. sirloin steak (1½" thick)
½   tsp. salt
1   Tbsp. coarsely ground black pepper
2   Tbsp. olive oil
1   (7-oz.) jar refrigerated pesto
1   (7-oz.) jar roasted red bell peppers, drained and
     chopped
1   Tbsp. lemon juice

Sprinkle both sides of steak with salt and 1 Tbsp. pepper; brush with olive oil. Place grill pan over medium-high heat until hot. Cook steak in hot grill pan 5 to 7 minutes on each side or until desired degree of doneness. Transfer steak to a carving board, and let stand 5 minutes.

Meanwhile, combine pesto, chopped roasted red pepper, and lemon juice in a small bowl.

Cut steak into thin slices, and transfer to a serving platter. Serve with red pepper pesto. **Yield: 4 to 6 servings.**

Sausage Italian Bread Pizza

Sausage Italian Bread Pizza

Choose your favorite sauce for this quick pizza. Most supermarkets have a good selection of jarred pasta and pizza sauces ranging in flavor from simple marinara to roasted pepper.

Prep: 12 min.   Cook: 19 min.

1   lb. mild or hot Italian sausage
2   Tbsp. olive oil, divided
1   onion, halved and thinly sliced
2   garlic cloves, minced
1   cup pizza or pasta sauce
1½ tsp. dried oregano
¼   tsp. dried crushed red pepper
¼   tsp. salt
1   (1-lb.) loaf semolina bread (about 14" long)
⅔   cup ricotta cheese, divided
2   cups (8 oz.) shredded mozzarella cheese, divided
¼   cup grated Parmesan cheese, divided

Remove and discard casings from sausage. Cook sausage in a large skillet over medium-high heat 8 minutes, stirring until meat crumbles and is no longer pink. Push meat to outer edges of pan; add 1 Tbsp. oil. Add onion and garlic; cook 5 minutes or until onion is softened. Remove from heat; stir in pizza sauce and next 3 ingredients.

Cut bread in half lengthwise using a serrated knife, and scoop out center of each bread half, leaving a ½" border; discard scooped-out bread or reserve for making breadcrumbs.

Spread ⅓ cup ricotta down center of each bread half. Top each evenly with sausage mixture, mozzarella, and Parmesan cheese. Drizzle pizzas evenly with remaining 1 Tbsp. oil. Place pizzas on a lightly greased baking sheet.

Bake at 425° for 6 minutes or until cheese is melted and pizzas are thoroughly heated. **Yield: 4 servings.**

Monterey Jack Omelets with Bacon, Avocado, and Salsa

Omelets make wonderful quick suppers. This southwestern-flavored omelet makes two hefty servings or serves four if you'd like.

Prep: 9 min.   Cook: 7 min.

6   fully cooked bacon slices
1   cup (4 oz.) shredded Monterey Jack cheese, divided
1   avocado, diced
¼   cup bottled salsa
¼   cup minced fresh cilantro
6   large eggs
2   Tbsp. water
½   tsp. salt
¼   tsp. freshly ground black pepper
¼   cup butter, divided

Reheat bacon according to package directions until crisp; coarsely crumble. Stir together bacon, ½ cup cheese, avocado, and salsa; set aside to use as filling. Combine remaining ½ cup cheese and cilantro in a bowl.

Whisk together eggs, water, salt, and pepper. Melt 2 Tbsp. butter in a 9" nonstick skillet over medium-high heat. Pour half of egg mixture into skillet, and sprinkle with half of cilantro-cheese mixture. As egg starts to cook, gently lift edges of omelet with a spatula, and tilt pan so uncooked portion flows underneath. Sprinkle 1 side of omelet with half of bacon filling. Fold in half. Cook over medium-low heat 45 seconds. Remove from pan, and keep warm. Repeat procedure with remaining butter, egg mixture, cilantro-cheese mixture, and bacon filling. Serve hot. **Yield: 2 servings.**

Chicken with Cranberry Mojo

Prep: 9 min.   Cook: 6 min.

1   tsp. salt
1   tsp. ground cumin
½   tsp. ground coriander
¼   tsp. freshly ground black pepper
6   skinned and boned chicken breasts
2   Tbsp. olive oil
Cranberry Mojo

Combine first 4 ingredients in a small bowl; set aside. Place chicken breasts between 2 sheets of heavy-duty plastic wrap, and flatten to ¼" thickness using a meat mallet or rolling pin.

Sprinkle chicken with spice mixture. Cook chicken in hot oil in a large nonstick skillet over medium heat 2 to 3 minutes on each side or until done. Serve with Cranberry Mojo. **Yield: 4 servings.**

Cranberry Mojo

2   cups fresh cranberries
½   cup frozen cranberry juice concentrate, thawed
¼   cup fresh cilantro leaves
2   Tbsp. olive oil
1   Tbsp. fresh lime juice
1   Tbsp. honey
1   garlic clove, sliced
¼   tsp. ground cumin
¼   tsp. salt

Combine all ingredients in a food processor; pulse 3 times or until mixture is coarsely chopped. Serve over chicken. **Yield: 1½ cups.**

Cranberry Chicken Salad Empanadas

Look for a premium, freshly made deli chicken salad, or use leftover holiday turkey. One empanada makes the perfect appetizer; two with a small salad fit the entrée bill.

Prep: 10 min.   Cook: 16 min.

1   (15-oz.) package refrigerated piecrusts
1   cup deli chicken salad
⅓   cup sweetened dried cranberries
⅓   cup pecan pieces, toasted
1   large egg, lightly beaten

Working with 1 crust at a time, unroll piecrust according to package directions onto a lightly floured surface. Cut each piecrust into 4 (4½") circles.

Combine chicken salad, cranberries, and pecans in a bowl. Spoon about 2 Tbsp. chicken salad mixture in center of each circle. Brush edges of circles with beaten egg. Fold dough over filling for each empanada, pressing edges with a fork to seal. Place empanadas onto a lightly greased baking sheet, and brush with beaten egg. Repeat procedure with remaining piecrust circles, chicken salad mixture, and beaten egg.

Bake at 400° for 16 minutes or until lightly browned. Serve warm or at room temperature. **Yield: 8 empanadas.**

Cranberry Parfaits

quick & easy

Cranberry Parfaits

Prep: 22 min.

1¼ cups fresh or frozen cranberries
½ cup light corn syrup
1 tsp. grated orange rind
1 cup whipping cream
1 cup sifted powdered sugar
1½ cups sour cream
½ tsp. vanilla extract
Garnish: cranberries cut in half

Process 1¼ cups cranberries and corn syrup in a food processor until finely chopped. Transfer to a small bowl, and stir in orange rind.

Beat whipping cream until foamy; gradually add powdered sugar, beating until stiff peaks form.

Stir together sour cream and vanilla extract in a medium bowl. Fold in half of whipped cream. Fold in remaining whipped cream.

Spoon about 1 Tbsp. cranberry syrup into each of 6 parfait glasses; top with about ⅓ cup sour cream mixture. Repeat layers once. Garnish, if desired. **Yield: 6 servings.**

Ginger Streusel-Topped Cheesecake

This easy dressed-up cheesecake is topped with big chunks of crunchy gingersnap streusel. Serve it warm from the oven, and scoop it into dessert bowls.

Prep: 5 min.   Cook: 19 min.

1	cup coarsely crushed gingersnaps (we tested with Nabisco)
½	cup butter, softened
½	cup sugar
½	cup all-purpose flour
1	Tbsp. finely chopped crystallized ginger
1	(30-oz.) frozen New York style cheesecake (we tested with Sara Lee)

Ginger Streusel-Topped Pumpkin Pie

Combine first 5 ingredients, mixing well with a spoon. Sprinkle streusel over top of frozen cheesecake. Bake at 425° for 16 to 19 minutes or until streusel is browned. Scoop warm cheesecake into serving bowls. **Yield: 8 servings.**

Ginger Streusel-Topped Pumpkin Pie: Prepare topping as directed for cheesecake. Sprinkle topping over a small deli-baked pumpkin pie. Bake again at 425° for 18 to 20 minutes to brown the streusel. Let stand 15 minutes. Slice to serve. **Yield: 8 servings.**

▲ This frozen cheesecake comes wrapped in a collar. Just top the cheesecake with homemade streusel and pop it in the oven to bake the streusel.

Ginger Streusel-Topped Cheesecake

Cheesecake-Stuffed Dark Chocolate Cake

Though it isn't ready in 30 minutes, there's a lot that is express about this grand cake. It's even better once you've chilled it. (also pictured on page 60)

Prep: 26 min.   Cook: 32 min.   Other: 1 hr., 10 min.

Unsweetened cocoa
1   (18.25-oz.) package devil's food cake mix
1   (3.4-oz.) package chocolate instant pudding mix
3   large eggs
1¼   cups milk
1   cup canola oil
1   Tbsp. vanilla extract
1½   tsp. chocolate extract (optional)
1   tsp. almond extract
3   (1.55-oz.) milk chocolate bars, chopped (we tested with Hershey's)
3   (16-oz.) cans homestyle cream cheese frosting
3   (7.75-oz.) boxes frozen cheesecake bites, coarsely chopped (we tested with Sara Lee)
1   (12-oz.) jar dulce de leche caramel sauce (we tested with Smucker's)
Double chocolate rolled wafer cookies, coarsely broken (we tested with Pirouline)
Chocolate fudge rolled wafer cookies, coarsely broken (we tested with Pepperidge Farm)

Grease 2 (9") round cakepans, and dust with cocoa.

Beat cake mix and next 7 ingredients at low speed with an electric mixer 1 minute; then beat at medium speed 2 minutes. Fold in chopped milk chocolate bars. Pour batter into prepared pans.

Bake at 350° for 32 minutes or until cake springs back when lightly touched. Cool cake in pans on wire racks 10 minutes; remove from pans, and cool completely on wire racks. Wrap and chill cake layers at least 1 hour or up to 24 hours. (This step enables you to split cake layers with ease.)

Using a serrated knife, slice cake layers in half horizontally to make 4 layers. Place 1 layer, cut side up, on a cake plate. Spread with ½ cup cream cheese frosting; sprinkle with one-fourth of chopped cheesecake bites. Repeat procedure with remaining 3 layers, frosting, and cheesecake bites, omitting cheesecake bites on top of last layer. Frost sides and top of cake with remaining frosting. Drizzle desired amount of caramel sauce over cake, letting it drip down sides. Chill until ready to serve. Decorate cake with rolled wafer cookies and remaining chopped cheesecake bites. Store in refrigerator. **Yield: 12 servings.**

This impressive dessert makes the most of cake mix, canned frosting, frozen cheesecake bites, and a jar of caramel sauce.

Cheesecake-Stuffed
Dark Chocolate
Cake

◀ Sprinkle chopped cheesecake bites over each frosted cake layer.

Make-Ahead
Party Food

These scrumptious do-ahead dishes have broad
appeal, hefty yields, and big flavor.

Deviled Eggs with Smoked Salmon and Cream Cheese

Hard-cooked eggs get dolled up with the classic combination of smoked salmon and cream cheese. If you're buying smoked salmon for a special occasion, set aside some for this hors d'oeuvre.

Prep: 18 min.   Cook: 8 min.   Other: 15 min.

6   large eggs
3   Tbsp. minced smoked salmon (about 1 oz.)
3   Tbsp. minced green onions
3   Tbsp. softened cream cheese
1   Tbsp. sour cream
1   tsp. Dijon mustard
2   tsp. lemon juice
¼   tsp. salt
⅛   tsp. ground red pepper
Garnishes: fresh dill, smoked salmon slivers, sweet paprika

Place eggs and enough water to cover in a saucepan over medium heat; bring to a boil. Cover, remove from heat, and let stand 15 minutes. Drain; return eggs to saucepan, and add enough cold water and ice to cover. Let cool. Remove shells from eggs, halve each egg lengthwise, and scrape yolks into a bowl. Reserve egg whites.

Combine yolks, salmon, and next 7 ingredients, mashing with a fork until well blended. Spoon filling into reserved whites, cover loosely with plastic wrap, and refrigerate up to 2 days. Garnish, if desired. **Yield: 12 servings.**

Southwestern Spinach Dip

Prep: 10 min.

⅔   cup mayonnaise
½   (8-oz.) package cream cheese, softened
½   cup fresh cilantro leaves
2   Tbsp. sliced green onions
1   tsp. grated lime rind
2   Tbsp. fresh lime juice
½   tsp. ground cumin
½   tsp. salt
1   jalapeño pepper, seeded and chopped
1   (10-oz.) package frozen chopped spinach, thawed and squeezed dry

Combine first 9 ingredients in a food processor; process until smooth. Add spinach, and pulse 3 times or until

blended. Transfer dip to a bowl; cover and refrigerate up to 1 day. Serve with fresh cut vegetables, multigrain tortilla chips, or crackers. **Yield: 1½ cups.**

Honey-Peppered Goat Cheese with Fig Balsamic Drizzle

Prep: 8 min.

1   (11-oz.) package or 4 (3-oz.) logs fresh goat cheese
⅓   cup olive oil
¼   cup honey
½   tsp. freshly ground black pepper
1   tsp. fresh thyme leaves
Fig balsamic vinegar* or balsamic vinegar
Garnish: fresh thyme
Lahvosh or other cracker bread

Using a sharp knife, carefully slice goat cheese in ½"-thick slices. Place cheese in an 11" x 7" dish or other serving platter. Drizzle with oil. Combine honey and pepper; drizzle over cheese. Sprinkle with 1 tsp. thyme leaves. Cover and chill up to 2 days.

Remove cheese from refrigerator 1 hour before serving. Just before serving, drizzle a little vinegar over cheese. Garnish, if desired. Serve with lahvosh or other specialty cracker bread. **Yield: 6 to 8 appetizer servings.**

*Find fig balsamic vinegar at Williams-Sonoma or other cook stores.

Honey-Peppered Goat Cheese with Fig Balsamic Drizzle

Mediterranean Mezze

Mezze are small plates of food served midday in Greece and other Mediterranean countries. Although traditionally meant to be eaten as a nosh with drinks, these little plates make wonderful hors d'oeuvres. Variety is the key word here and, in addition to the 3 recipes that follow, the Mezze table can be augmented with store-bought items such as black and green olives, cheese, roasted red peppers, nuts (pistachios and almonds), pepperoncini (pickled Tuscan peppers), and, of course, pita bread.

editor's favorite • make ahead • quick & easy

Hummus

This version of hummus was such a hit that we gave it our highest rating.

Prep: 7 min.

1	(19-oz.) can chickpeas (garbanzo beans)
2	garlic cloves, chopped
⅓	cup extra-virgin olive oil
⅓	cup water
⅓	cup fresh lemon juice
⅓	cup tahini*
½	tsp. salt
1	Tbsp. extra-virgin olive oil
2	Tbsp. minced fresh flat-leaf parsley
2	Tbsp. pine nuts, toasted

Pita bread, cut into wedges

Combine first 7 ingredients in a food processor; process until smooth. Transfer hummus to a serving bowl; cover and refrigerate up to 5 days before serving.

To serve, drizzle hummus with 1 Tbsp. olive oil, and sprinkle with parsley and toasted pine nuts. Serve with pita wedges. **Yield: 2 cups.**

*Tahini is a popular ingredient used in Middle Eastern cooking. It's a thick paste made from ground sesame seeds. Tahini can be found with the peanut butter or with organic foods at your grocer.

editor's favorite • make ahead

Babaghanouj

This dip (pronounced bah-bah-gah-NOOSH) gets wonderful smoky flavor from two sources—grilled eggplant and smoked paprika. Look for smoked paprika at specialty food stores or spice stores. It's one of those secret ingredients that turns an ordinary dish into an extraordinary one. Of course, you can make it with regular paprika, but you won't have the same smoky essence. This dip is best made ahead, as the flavors tend to mellow.

Prep: 15 min.   Cook: 14 min.   Other: 40 min.

Olive oil-flavored cooking spray

1	medium eggplant, cut in half lengthwise (about 1 lb.)
2	Tbsp. extra-virgin olive oil
2	large garlic cloves, chopped
2	Tbsp. tahini
2	Tbsp. fresh lemon juice
1	Tbsp. sour cream
½	tsp. salt
⅛	tsp. ground red pepper

Extra-virgin olive oil
Smoked paprika
Pitted kalamata olives, halved
Pita chips

Spray cut sides of eggplant with cooking spray. Grill eggplant, skin side down, covered with grill lid, over medium-high heat (350° to 400°) 10 minutes. Turn eggplant halves over, and grill 4 minutes or until flesh is nicely browned and tender. Remove from grill, and let stand 20 minutes or until cool to the touch.

Scoop pulp from eggplant halves into a large wire-mesh strainer; let drain 20 minutes. Combine drained pulp, 2 Tbsp. olive oil, and next 6 ingredients in a food processor. Process until smooth. Transfer to a bowl; cover and refrigerate up to 1 week.

To serve, transfer dip to a serving bowl; drizzle with a small amount of olive oil, and sprinkle with smoked paprika and olives. Serve with pita chips. **Yield: 1⅔ cups.**

Tzatziki

This refreshing cucumber yogurt dip can be served as part of the traditional Mezze (see note at far left), but it's also perfect as a sauce for poached salmon or other cold seafood. Be sure to look for Greek yogurt. It's thick, rich, and predrained. Plain yogurt can be substituted; see note below.

Prep: 16 min.

2   large cucumbers, peeled, seeded, and grated (about 1¼ pounds unpeeled)
2   cups Greek yogurt or 4 cups plain yogurt, drained (see note)
2   garlic cloves, minced
3   Tbsp. fresh lemon juice
1½   Tbsp. chopped fresh dill
1½   Tbsp. chopped fresh mint
½   tsp. salt

Press grated cucumber between layers of paper towels to remove excess moisture. Stir together cucumber, yogurt, and remaining ingredients. Cover and refrigerate up to 5 days. **Yield: 2¾ cups.**

Note: To drain plain yogurt, line a sieve with a double thickness of cheesecloth; set sieve over a bowl. Spoon yogurt into sieve, and let drain in refrigerator at least 3 hours.

Peach and Pecan Tapenade with Goat Cheese

We gave this traditional French condiment a Southern twist with pecans and dried peaches. The result is a beautiful spread that's sure to impress.

Prep: 8 min.   Cook: 9 min.   Other: 30 min.

1   cup orange juice
2   cups dried peaches, chopped (we tested with Sunmaid)
1   cup pitted kalamata olives, chopped
2   Tbsp. olive oil
2   Tbsp. honey
1   Tbsp. capers, drained
½   tsp. dried thyme
¼   tsp. freshly ground pepper
1   cup chopped pecans, toasted
12   oz. goat cheese
Specialty crackers

Peach and Pecan Tapenade with Goat Cheese

Bring orange juice to a boil in a small saucepan over medium heat. Remove from heat, and add chopped dried peaches. Cover and let stand 30 minutes. Drain, if necessary.

Combine olives and next 5 ingredients in a serving bowl. Stir in peaches and pecans. Place tapenade on a serving platter with goat cheese and crackers. Spread cheese on crackers, and smear with tapenade. **Yield: 3¾ cups.**

Make Ahead: Prepare tapenade, omitting nuts. Cover and store in refrigerator up to 2 days. Stir in nuts just before serving.

Bourbon BBQ Baby Back Ribs

Prebaking these ribs gives them a rich browned exterior. The subsequent long, slow stint in the slow cooker produces fall-off-the-bone, fork-tender ribs.

Prep: 10 min.   Cook: 10 hr., 9 min.   Other: 30 min.

5	lb. pork baby back ribs, racks cut in half
1½	tsp. salt
1	tsp. pepper
1	cup ketchup
1	cup firmly packed light brown sugar
½	cup bourbon
¼	cup prepared horseradish
½	tsp. hot sauce

Place ribs, meaty-side up, in a large roasting pan. Sprinkle ribs with salt and pepper.

Bake at 475° for 30 minutes. Meanwhile, combine ketchup and next 4 ingredients in a small bowl.

Arrange ribs in a 6-qt. slow cooker, adding sauce on each layer of ribs. Depending on the shape of your slow cooker—oval or round—you may have to cut each rib rack into thirds instead of in half. Cover and cook ribs on LOW 9 hours. Remove ribs from slow cooker; cover to keep warm.

Pour drippings and sauce from slow cooker into a saucepan. (Skim a few ice cubes across the surface of sauce to remove fat, if desired, and discard.) Bring sauce to a boil; reduce heat, and simmer over medium heat 20 minutes or until sauce thickens. (Sauce will reduce by about half.) Brush sauce over ribs before serving. **Yield: 5 servings.**

Make Ahead: These ribs can hold for several hours after finishing in the slow cooker. Place sauced-up ribs on a rimmed baking sheet; cover tightly with foil. Place in a preheated 190° oven to keep warm.

Bourbon BBQ
Baby Back Ribs

You might not consider ribs as holiday food for entertaining, but this lip-smacking recipe will make you think twice.

▲ Arrange ribs in a single layer in a large roasting pan.

Boeuf Bourguignon

We almost insist you make this beef stew a day ahead and just reheat when ready to serve. The rich flavors meld together and only get better with time. One key to success: Be sure to brown the beef well. Do this in batches in a very hot pan—this creates an intense layer of flavor that will permeate the dish.

Prep: 12 min.   Cook: 4 hr.   Other: 8 hr.

2½	cups Cabernet Sauvignon or other dry red wine
2	cups beef broth
2	Tbsp. fresh rosemary leaves
3	Tbsp. minced garlic
4	lb. boneless beef chuck roast, cut into 2" pieces and well trimmed
6	oz. thick-sliced bacon, cut into ½" pieces
2	cups beef broth
¼	cup olive oil
1	(8-oz.) package small button mushrooms, halved
1½	tsp. salt, divided
1	(1-lb.) package frozen pearl onions, thawed and drained
5	carrots, peeled and cut into 2" pieces
3	Tbsp. cornstarch
¼	cup water

Salt and pepper to taste
Minced fresh flat-leaf parsley

Combine first 4 ingredients in a large zip-top freezer bag. Add beef, and seal bag; refrigerate overnight. Drain meat and aromatics, reserving liquid. Pat meat dry with paper towels.

Cook bacon in a large Dutch oven over medium heat 8 minutes or until crisp. Drain bacon on paper towels, and set aside; reserve drippings in pan.

Add meat to Dutch oven in 3 batches, and cook without crowding meat 10 to 15 minutes per batch or until well browned; set aside. Pour off any remaining bacon drippings; return browned meat and reserved marinade to Dutch oven, and add 2 cups broth. Bring mixture to a boil; reduce heat, and simmer, partially covered, 2 hours and 45 minutes or until meat is tender.

Meanwhile, heat 2 Tbsp. oil in a large nonstick skillet over medium-high heat until hot. Add mushrooms and ¼ tsp. salt; cook 12 to 15 minutes or until browned, stirring after 10 minutes. Set mushrooms aside. Heat remaining 2 Tbsp. oil in same skillet; add onions, carrots, and ¼ tsp. salt, and cook 10 minutes or until golden brown, stirring often. Add mushrooms, onions, and carrots to meat in Dutch oven. Stir in 1 tsp. salt. Continue simmering stew 15 minutes or until vegetables are tender.

Combine cornstarch and water; stir into stew, and cook 3 to 5 minutes or until thickened. Add salt and pepper to taste. Sprinkle with bacon and parsley before serving. **Yield: 8 servings.**

Note: You can prepare the beef stew, cool it completely, and keep it refrigerated up to 3 days.

Meat Lover's Chili

This chili is better the second and even third day, but feel free to enjoy it freshly made with minced red onion, shredded Monterey Jack cheese, chopped fresh cilantro, sour cream, and a basket of warm flour tortillas.

Prep: 17 min.   Cook: 1 hr., 21 min.

3	lb. ground chuck
3	medium onions, chopped
1	large green bell pepper, chopped
3	Tbsp. minced garlic
½	cup chili powder
1	Tbsp. ground cumin
1	(14-oz.) can beef broth
1	Tbsp. dried oregano
1½	tsp. salt
2	(28-oz.) cans diced tomatoes, undrained
3	(15-oz.) cans pinto beans, rinsed and drained

Brown beef in a large Dutch oven over medium heat. Drain beef, reserving ¼ cup drippings in pan.

Add onion, bell pepper, and garlic to drippings; sauté over medium-high heat 6 to 8 minutes or until vegetables are tender. Return beef to Dutch oven.

Stir in chili powder and cumin; cook over medium heat 3 minutes, stirring occasionally. Stir in beef broth and next 3 ingredients. Reduce heat, and simmer, covered, 50 minutes, stirring occasionally. Add pinto beans, and cook 20 more minutes. **Yield: 16 cups.**

Tortilla Chicken Casserole

Get a jump start on dinner with this southwestern comfort food casserole that can be made up to 2 days ahead. Serve with an array of toppings: diced avocado, sour cream, lime wedges, sliced pickled jalapeño, fresh cilantro, and salsa.

Prep: 17 min.   Cook: 1 hr.

3	Tbsp. vegetable oil
1½	cups minced red bell pepper
1½	cups minced onion
2	Tbsp. minced garlic
½	tsp. salt
2½	tsp. ground cumin
¼	cup all-purpose flour
1½	cups chicken broth
1	cup sour cream
5	cups chopped cooked chicken or turkey
12	corn tortillas
3	cups (12 oz.) shredded Monterey Jack cheese

Heat oil in a large nonstick skillet over medium heat until hot. Add bell pepper and next 3 ingredients; sauté 5 minutes or until vegetables are soft. Stir in cumin, and cook 1 minute. Stir in flour; cook 3 minutes. Add chicken broth and sour cream; simmer 5 minutes, stirring frequently. Add chicken, and stir to blend.

Soften tortillas by layering them between damp paper towels and heating in microwave, in several batches, at HIGH for 30 seconds.

Arrange 4 tortillas in a lightly greased 3-qt. baking dish. Top with one-third of chicken mixture (about 2 cups), sprinkle with 1 cup cheese, and cover with 4 more tortillas. Repeat layers with another one-third of chicken mixture, 1 cup cheese, 4 tortillas, and ending with remaining chicken and 1 cup cheese. Cover with aluminum foil, and refrigerate up to 2 days.

Bake, uncovered, at 350° for 35 to 45 minutes or until bubbling and browned. **Yield: 8 servings.**

Note: You can also freeze this casserole. Follow the make-ahead directions above but freeze after preparing. When ready to cook it, bake foil-covered frozen casserole at 350° for 1 hour and 15 minutes or until thoroughly heated.

Chicken à la King

A classic American dish evoking childhood memories for some of us, Chicken à la King is elegant enough for a party buffet, and yet comfort food at its best. Serve the creamy chicken over our Crisp Cheddar-Cornmeal Waffles, and it'll be a hit. The dish can be prepared 2 days ahead, stored covered, and chilled.

Prep: 25 min.   Cook: 1 hr.

4	cups chicken broth
2	lb. skinned and boned chicken breasts
6	Tbsp. butter, divided
4	red bell peppers, diced ½"
1	medium onion, diced ½"
1	(8-oz.) package fresh mushrooms, quartered
1	tsp. salt
⅛	tsp. ground red pepper
6	Tbsp. all-purpose flour
2	cups whipping cream
3	Tbsp. dry sherry
2	Tbsp. lemon juice

Salt and pepper to taste
Crisp Cheddar-Cornmeal Waffles
Garnishes: toasted sliced almonds, flat-leaf parsley

Pour broth in a Dutch oven or stockpot; bring to a boil. Add chicken; reduce heat to medium-low, and cook, uncovered, 10 minutes. Remove chicken from broth; coarsely chop, and set aside. Strain broth through a sieve into a saucepan; simmer, uncovered, over medium heat until reduced to 2½ cups (10 to 20 minutes).

Melt 3 Tbsp. butter in a large skillet over medium heat. Sauté red bell pepper and onion 4 minutes or until tender. Add mushrooms, salt, and ground red pepper; sauté 4 minutes. Remove from heat, and set aside.

While broth continues to simmer, preheat waffle iron, and cook waffles.

Melt remaining 3 Tbsp. butter in Dutch oven over low heat; whisk in flour until smooth. Cook 3 minutes, whisking constantly. Gradually whisk in reserved 2½ cups broth and cream; cook over medium heat, whisking constantly, until sauce is thickened and bubbly.

Add chicken and reserved vegetables to sauce. Stir in sherry and lemon juice; cook over medium heat, just until thoroughly heated. Add salt and pepper to taste. Serve over waffles. Garnish, if desired. **Yield: 12 cups.**

Chicken à la King with Crisp Cheddar-Cornmeal Waffles

Crisp Cheddar-Cornmeal Waffles

Prep: 12 min. Cook: 10 min. per batch

These waffles are crisp and interesting on their own or with syrup, but crown them with some Chicken à la King and they become fancy brunch fare.

1 cup all-purpose flour
1 cup yellow cornmeal
2 tsp. baking powder
1 tsp. baking soda
½ tsp. salt
1½ cups (6 oz.) shredded sharp Cheddar cheese
½ cup chopped toasted pecans
3 large eggs
1 cup buttermilk
1 cup club soda
⅓ cup canola or vegetable oil

Sift together first 5 ingredients in a large bowl. Stir in cheese and pecans. Combine eggs and next 3 ingredients; gently stir into dry ingredients just until blended.

Spoon a heaping 1 cup batter evenly onto a preheated, lightly greased waffle iron. Cook 5 to 10 minutes or until crisp and done. Repeat with remaining batter.

Transfer waffles to a baking sheet, and keep warm, uncovered, in the oven at 200° until ready to serve. Waffles can be frozen in zip-top freezer bags and reheated in oven or toaster oven. **Yield: 16 (4") waffles.**

Note: To make Belgian waffles, spoon 2 cups batter into a preheated, greased Belgian waffle iron with 4 square grids. Cook until crisp and done.

Twice-Baked Smoky Sweet Potatoes

Like a twice-baked potato, this sweet potato version mashes yummy ingredients together and then gets a crusty cheese topping with a surprise ingredient. The results pair well with pork tenderloin, turkey, or ham.

Prep: 21 min.   Cook: 1 hr., 12 min.

6	medium sweet potatoes (3½ lb.)
⅓	cup butter or margarine
½	cup whipping cream, half-and-half, or milk
¼	tsp. salt
¼	tsp. smoked paprika
⅛	tsp. ground red pepper
½	cup crushed amaretti cookies (about 4 cookies)
¼	tsp. smoked paprika
¾	cup grated Parmigiano-Reggiano cheese

Scrub potatoes, and prick each potato once. Place on a baking sheet. Bake at 450° for 1 hour or until tender.

When potatoes are cool enough to handle, cut a strip from top of each potato; carefully scoop out potato pulp, leaving ⅛"-thick shells. Set shells aside. Place pulp, butter, and next 4 ingredients in a medium bowl. Mash with a potato masher, or beat at medium speed with an electric mixer until smooth; spoon into potato shells. Cover and chill up to 2 days.

When ready to bake, place stuffed potatoes on a large, round microwave-safe, ovenproof platter, and cover with a paper towel. Microwave potatoes at HIGH 6 minutes or until thoroughly heated.

Combine crushed cookies, ¼ tsp. paprika, and cheese. Sprinkle over potatoes. Bake at 400° for 6 minutes or until browned. **Yield: 6 servings.**

Note: You can find smoked paprika at specialty grocery stores or spice stores.

Citrus Cheesecake

The beauty of pomegranate seeds nestled against sectioned oranges and candied orange peel gives this creamy cheesecake grande dame status. Baking it in a water bath makes it extra creamy.

Prep: 8 min.   Cook: 55 min.   Other: 8 hr.

4	navel oranges
¾	cup sugar
¾	cup water
¼	cup sugar
2	cups graham cracker crumbs
½	cup butter, melted
⅓	cup sugar
½	tsp. ground ginger
3	(8-oz.) packages cream cheese, softened
1¼	cups sugar
1	(8-oz.) container sour cream
4	large eggs
1	Tbsp. grated lemon rind
2	tsp. vanilla extract
1	tsp. orange extract
1	large pomegranate, seeds removed

Using a zester and working from top of orange to bottom, remove peel from oranges in long strips. Combine ¾ cup sugar and ¾ cup water in a small saucepan over medium-low heat, stirring until sugar dissolves. Bring to a boil; reduce heat, and simmer 2 minutes. Add orange peel; simmer 15 minutes.

Meanwhile, peel and section zested oranges. Seal orange sections in a zip-top plastic bag, and refrigerate until ready to garnish cheesecake.

Drain orange peel well. Toss with ¼ cup sugar in a small bowl. Place candied peel in a thin layer on wax paper to dry. Store in an airtight container up to 2 days.

Combine graham cracker crumbs and next 3 ingredients; stir well. Press mixture firmly on bottom and 2" up sides of a lightly greased 9" springform pan.

Bake at 350° for 14 to 16 minutes; let cool. Wrap bottom and sides of pan in aluminum foil and place in a large roasting pan; set aside. (Wrapping the pan is insurance against leaks in case your pan is older and not 100% airtight.)

Beat cream cheese at medium-high speed with an electric mixer until creamy. Gradually add 1¼ cups sugar, beating just until blended. Add sour cream, beating just until blended. Add eggs, 1 at a time, beating well after each addition. Stir in lemon rind and extracts.

Citrus Cheesecake

Pour batter into baked crust. Add hot water to roasting pan to a depth of 2". Bake at 350° for 55 minutes or until edges are set and center is almost set. Carefully remove pan from water bath, and immediately run a knife around edge of pan. Cool completely on a wire rack; cover and chill 8 hours.

To serve cheesecake, remove sides of springform pan. Place cheesecake on a serving platter. Arrange orange sections in concentric circles on top of cake. Pile pomegranate seeds in center of cheesecake. Decorate with candied orange peel. **Yield: 12 servings.**

▲ To make candied citrus peel, use a zester and work from top to bottom of fruit.

▲ Place candied peel in a thin layer to dry after it's been cooked and sugared.

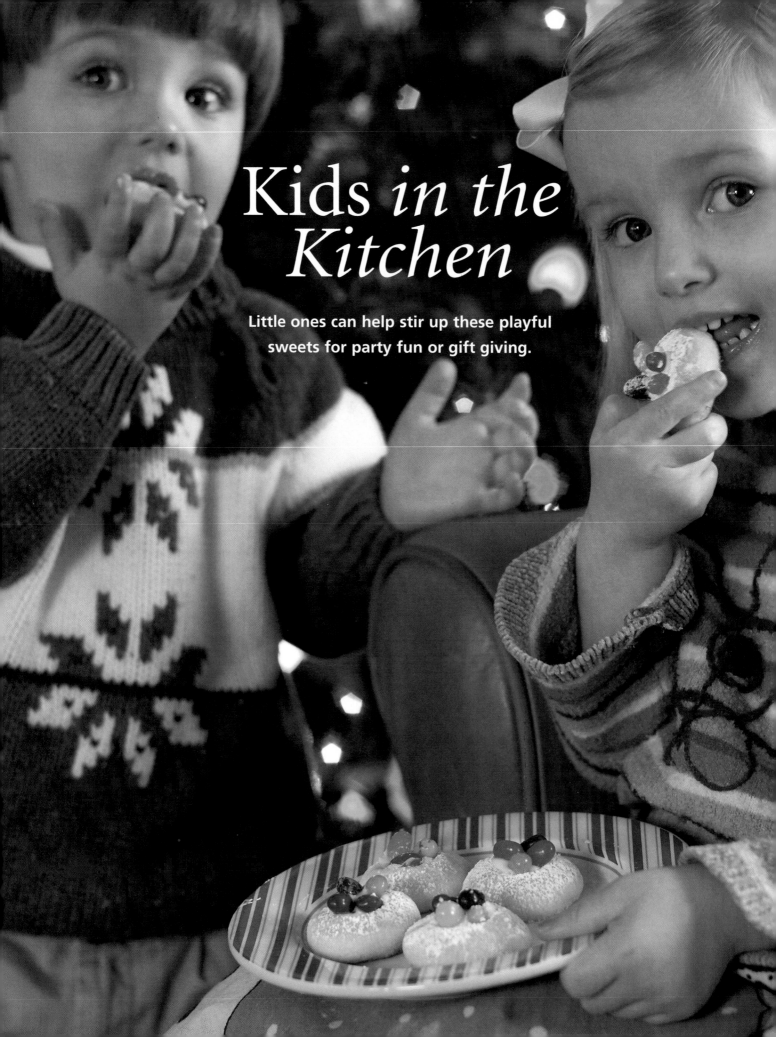

Kids *in the* Kitchen

Little ones can help stir up these playful
sweets for party fun or gift giving.

Jelly beans make a fun middle for these classic vanilla cookies.

make ahead
Jelly Bean Thumbprint Cookies

Prep: 6 min.   Cook: 13 min.   Other: 8 hr.

1   cup butter, softened
⅔   cup granulated sugar
2   egg yolks
1   tsp. vanilla extract
2¼   cups all-purpose flour
¼   tsp. salt
⅓   cup powdered sugar
2   Tbsp. heavy whipping cream
Assorted jelly beans
Additional powdered sugar

Beat butter at medium speed with an electric mixer until creamy; gradually add ⅔ cup sugar, beating well. Add egg yolks and vanilla, beating until blended.

Combine flour and salt; add to butter mixture, beating at low speed until blended. Cover and chill dough 8 hours.

Shape dough into 1" balls, and place 2" apart on ungreased baking sheets. Press thumb into each cookie to make an indentation.

Bake at 350° for 12 to 13 minutes. Cool 1 minute on baking sheets; remove to wire racks. Make thumbprint indentations again while cookies are still warm; let cookies cool completely.

Meanwhile, combine ⅓ cup powdered sugar and heavy cream in a small bowl; stir with a fork until smooth. Spoon icing into a zip-top freezer bag; cut a tiny hole in 1 corner of bag, and squirt a small amount of icing into indentation in each cookie. Press jelly beans into center of each cookie. Let set. Dust cookies with powdered sugar. **Yield: 1½ dozen.**

make ahead
Wreath Cookies

With only a few ingredients, you can transform shredded wheat cereal into these whimsical holiday wreaths. Let the kids help shape and decorate them.

Prep: 25 min.   Cook: 3 min.   Other: 30 min.

1   (12-oz.) package vanilla candy coating, broken up
Green paste food coloring
2½   cups coarsely crushed mini shredded whole wheat
        cereal biscuits (we tested with vanilla creme-flavored
        Frosted Mini Wheats)
Mini candy-coated chocolate pieces, red cinnamon
        candies, swirled holiday white morsels

Microwave vanilla candy coating in a medium bowl at MEDIUM (50% power) 3 minutes, stirring after every minute. Stir in desired amount of food coloring. Add cereal, stirring gently to coat. Drop cereal mixture by heaping tablespoonfuls onto wax paper; shape each spoonful into a wreath. Decorate with assorted candies. Let cookies stand about 30 minutes until firm. **Yield: about 1½ dozen.**

Wreath Cookies

Fudge Ring

Spooning this cookie- and candy-filled fudge into a home-made ring mold makes a fun project that the kids will want to take part in.

Prep: 10 min.   Cook: 12 min.   Other: 15 min.

1   (12-oz.) package milk chocolate morsels
1   cup butterscotch morsels
1   (14-oz.) can sweetened condensed milk
1   tsp. vanilla extract
Pinch of salt
Butter
1¼   cups candy-coated chocolate pieces
½   cup coarsely crushed cream-filled chocolate sandwich cookies (about 5 cookies)

Combine first 3 ingredients in a saucepan, reserving condensed milk can. Cook over medium-low heat until all morsels melt, stirring often. Remove from heat; stir in vanilla and salt. Cool slightly (about 15 minutes).

Meanwhile, grease an 8" round cake pan or springform pan with butter. Line pan with 2 pieces of plastic wrap, overlapping edges and smoothing out any wrinkles. Wrap empty condensed milk can with aluminum foil, smoothing out wrinkles; place in center of cake pan.

Stir 1 cup candies and crushed cookies into fudge; spread fudge in cake pan, holding can firmly in center. (A second pair of hands is a big help here.) Sprinkle remaining ¼ cup chocolate candies over fudge, gently pressing candies into fudge. Cover and chill until firm (about 2 to 3 hours).

To unmold, carefully loosen edges with a sharp knife, and remove can from center of fudge. Carefully invert fudge onto a plate. Invert again on a serving plate or cardboard cake round for gift giving. Cut fudge into thin slices to serve. **Yield: 2 lb.**

Note: For an easy gift giving "platter," we wrapped a cardboard cake round with wrapping paper.

Fudge Ring

▲ To unmold fudge, carefully loosen inside edges with a knife, and remove can.

▲ Lift fudge out of (springform) pan, peel away plastic wrap, and invert twice onto cardboard cake round.

Sugar Cookie Pops

You'll want to buy several containers of colored sugars and jimmies so you'll have plenty for coating these cookie balls.

Prep: 24 min.   Cook: 11 min. per batch   Other: 2 hr.

½   cup butter, softened
½   cup shortening
1   cup granulated sugar
1   cup powdered sugar
2   large eggs
¾   cup canola or vegetable oil
2   tsp. vanilla extract
4   cups all-purpose flour
1   tsp. baking soda
1   tsp. salt
1   tsp. cream of tartar
Colored sugars, sparkling sugars, and
      multicolored jimmies
4" white craft sticks

Beat butter and shortening at medium speed with an electric mixer until fluffy; add sugars, beating well. Add eggs, oil, and vanilla, beating until blended.

Combine flour and next 3 ingredients; add to butter mixture, blending well. Cover and chill dough 2 hours or overnight.

Shape dough into 1½" balls. Roll each ball in colored sugar or jimmies in individual bowls, pressing gently, if necessary, to coat balls. Place 2" apart on ungreased baking sheets. Insert craft sticks about 1" into each cookie to resemble a lollipop.

Bake at 350° for 10 to 11 minutes or until set. Let cool 2 minutes on baking sheets; remove cookie pops to wire racks to cool completely. **Yield: 4½ dozen.**

Tutti Fruity Crispy Candy

Tutti Fruity Crispy Candy

This simple candy recipe offers several opportunities for kids to help: Let them crush the pretzels in a zip-top plastic bag, stir the cereal into the melted vanilla coating, and, best of all, break the finished candy into pieces and sample it.

Prep: 5 min.   Cook: 2 min.   Other: 1 hr.

1   (24-oz.) package vanilla candy coating, broken up
2½   cups sweetened fruit-flavored multigrain cereal (we tested with Froot Loops)
1   cup thin pretzel sticks, coarsely broken

Line a lightly greased 15" x 10" jelly-roll pan with wax or parchment paper.

Melt candy coating in a large microwave-safe bowl according to package directions. Gently stir in cereal and pretzels. Spread candy onto wax paper. Let stand 1 hour or until firm. (Do not refrigerate.)

Break candy into pieces. Store in an airtight container. **Yield: about 1¾ lb.**

Peanut Butter 'n' Jelly Scones

Prep: 15 min.   Cook: 20 min.

3¼   cups all-purpose flour
⅔   cup firmly packed light brown sugar
1   Tbsp. baking powder
¾   tsp. salt
½   cup cold unsalted butter, cut into pieces
½   cup chunky peanut butter, chilled
½   cup semisweet chocolate morsels (optional)
⅔   cup whipping cream, divided
2   tsp. vanilla extract
2   Tbsp. turbinado sugar
About ¾ cup strawberry jelly

Combine first 4 ingredients in a food processor. Pulse briefly until combined. Add butter, and pulse to make a coarse meal. Add peanut butter, and pulse briefly to disperse evenly. Be careful not to overmix.

Transfer dough to a large bowl. Add chocolate morsels, if desired. Make a well in center, and add ½ cup plus 1 Tbsp. whipping cream and vanilla. Stir with a fork just until dry ingredients are moistened. Knead dough in bowl 2 or 3 times to incorporate dry ingredients in bottom of bowl.

Drop mounds of dough using a ⅓-cup measure onto a baking sheet lined with parchment paper. Smooth tops, and brush scones with remaining cream. Sprinkle with turbinado sugar. Make a deep indentation in center of each scone using thumb or the back of a small spoon; fill each with a scant tablespoon jelly.

Bake at 425° for 18 to 20 minutes or until scones are lightly browned around edges. Cool completely. **Yield: 1 dozen.**

Peanut Butter 'n' Jelly Scones

The classic kids' sandwich flavors are reinvented here as delectable tender scones. Let your little ones help spoon jelly onto the dough.

Our Top 10
Cookies & Brownies

Nearly a dozen all-time best, most decadent cookies, bars, and squares grace these pages.

Sparkling Ginger Stars

A heavy sugar crust and the peppery bite of fresh ginger make these gingerbread cookies scrumptious. Be sure your spices are fresh; it will make a big taste difference here.

Prep: 12 min.   Cook: 17 min. per batch   Other: 2 hr., 30 min.

1½	cups all-purpose flour
½	tsp. baking soda
½	tsp. salt
2	tsp. ground ginger
1	tsp. ground cinnamon
¼	tsp. ground cloves
¼	tsp. freshly grated nutmeg
½	cup unsalted butter, softened
½	cup firmly packed dark brown sugar
¼	cup dark molasses
1	egg yolk
1	Tbsp. grated lemon rind
1	Tbsp. grated fresh ginger
½	tsp. vanilla extract
1	large egg
2	Tbsp. whipping cream
1	(3.25-oz.) jar coarse sparkling sugar (see note)

Combine first 7 ingredients in a medium bowl; stir until blended.

Beat butter at medium speed with an electric mixer until creamy; gradually add brown sugar, beating well. Beat in molasses, egg yolk, lemon rind, grated ginger, and vanilla. Stir in flour mixture; beat just until blended.

Shape dough into a ball, and divide in half. Flatten each half into a round disk; wrap each in plastic wrap, and chill 2½ hours until firm.

Line 2 large baking sheets with parchment paper. Roll out dough, 1 section at a time, to ¼" thickness on a lightly floured surface. Cut into star shapes, using a 4" cookie cutter. Place ½" apart on prepared baking sheets.

Whisk together 1 egg and whipping cream; brush egg wash lightly over cookies. Sprinkle heavily with sparkling sugar.

Bake at 325° for 17 minutes or until cookies are puffed and slightly darker around edges. Cool 2 minutes on baking sheets; remove with parchment paper to wire racks to cool completely. **Yield: 2 dozen.**

Note: Sparkling sugar can be purchased at gourmet grocery stores or cake decorating shops, or ordered from La Cuisine at 800-521-1176 or lacuisineus.com.

Chunky Chocolate Gobs

editor's favorite

Chunky Chocolate Gobs

These ultrachocolate cookies are, hands down, some of the best ever to come through our test kitchen.

Prep: 18 min.   Cook: 12 min. per batch   Other: 30 min.

¾	cup unsalted butter, softened
⅓	cup butter-flavored shortening
1	cup granulated sugar
⅔	cup firmly packed dark brown sugar
2	large eggs
2	tsp. vanilla extract
2	cups all-purpose flour
⅔	cup unsweetened cocoa
1	tsp. baking soda
¼	tsp. salt
2	cups cream-filled chocolate sandwich cookies, coarsely chopped (16 cookies)
3	(1.75-oz.) Mounds bars, chilled and chopped
1	to 2 cups semisweet chocolate morsels

Beat butter and shortening at medium speed with an electric mixer until creamy; gradually add sugars, beating until light and fluffy. Add eggs and vanilla, beating until blended.

Combine flour and next 3 ingredients; gradually add to butter mixture, beating until blended. Stir in cookies, candy bars, and desired amount of chocolate morsels. Chill dough 30 minutes.

Drop dough by ¼ cupfuls 2" apart onto baking sheets lined with parchment paper. Bake at 350° for 10 to 12 minutes or until barely set. Cool on baking sheets 10 minutes. Transfer to wire racks to cool completely. **Yield: about 2½ dozen.**

Peppermint Bonbon Cookies

Peppermint Bonbon Cookies

Here's a decadent holiday combination—soft and chewy chocolate on the inside with a little peppermint candy crunch on top. These gems are great plain or we offer a double glaze option, too.

Prep: 25 min.   Cook: 13 min. per batch   Other: 2 hr., 35 min.

8	oz. bittersweet or semisweet chocolate, chopped
½	cup unsalted butter
1½	oz. unsweetened chocolate, chopped
½	cup finely crushed hard peppermint candies
6	Tbsp. granulated sugar
3	large eggs
1	tsp. vanilla extract
1	tsp. peppermint extract
1½	cups all-purpose flour
¾	tsp. baking powder
¼	tsp. salt
½	cup semisweet chocolate morsels

Additional coarsely crushed hard peppermint candies, divided

½	cup powdered sugar (optional)
2½	tsp. milk (optional)
½	cup semisweet chocolate morsels, melted (optional)

Combine first 3 ingredients in a large saucepan; cook over low heat until chocolate melts and mixture is smooth, stirring occasionally. Remove from heat, and stir in ½ cup crushed peppermint and 6 Tbsp. sugar. Let cool 30 minutes.

Add eggs to melted chocolate, 1 at a time, stirring well. Stir in extracts.

Combine flour, baking powder, and salt; add to chocolate mixture, stirring until combined. Stir in chocolate morsels. Cover and chill dough 2 hours or until firm enough to shape.

Shape dough into 1½" balls; place on parchment paper-lined baking sheets. Bake at 325° for 12 to 13 minutes or until cookies are puffed and cracked on top. Sprinkle coarsely crushed peppermints onto cookies; press candy lightly into cookies. Let cookies cool 5 minutes on baking sheets. Transfer to wire rack to cool completely.

Whisk together powdered sugar and milk; drizzle over cooled cookies, if desired. Drizzle with melted chocolate, if desired. Sprinkle cookies again with chopped peppermint, if desired. Let cookies stand until glaze and chocolate are firm. **Yield: about 2½ dozen.**

Crunchy Frostbite Cookies

Prep: 22 min.   Cook: 14 min. per batch   Other: 1 hr.

2	cups all-purpose flour
2	tsp. baking soda
1	tsp. baking powder
¼	tsp. salt
1	cup shortening
¾	cup granulated sugar
¾	cup firmly packed light brown sugar
2	large eggs
1	tsp. vanilla extract
1½	cups uncooked regular oats
1½	cups cornflakes cereal
12	oz. white chocolate baking squares, chopped
3	Tbsp. shortening
½	tsp. peppermint extract

Combine flour, baking soda, baking powder, and salt; stir well until blended.

Beat 1 cup shortening at medium speed with an electric mixer until creamy; gradually add sugars, beating well. Add eggs and vanilla; beat well. Add flour mixture, mixing just until blended. Stir in oats and cornflakes.

Drop dough by heaping tablespoonfuls, 2" apart, onto lightly greased baking sheets; flatten slightly. Bake at 325° for 12 to 14 minutes. Cool slightly on baking sheets. Transfer cookies to wire racks to cool completely.

Microwave white chocolate and 3 Tbsp. shortening in a medium-size microwave-safe bowl at HIGH 1 minute or until white chocolate melts, stirring once. Stir in peppermint extract. Dip flat bottom of each cookie into melted white chocolate, letting excess drip back into bowl. Place dipped cookies, dipped side up, on wax paper; let stand 1 hour or until white chocolate sets. **Yield: about 3 dozen.**

Crunchy Frostbite Cookies

editor's favorite • make ahead

White Chocolate-Oatmeal-Raisin Cookies

Using fiori di sicilia, an Italian citrus and vanilla flavoring, gives these easy drop cookies a subtle taste of orange.

Prep: 10 min.   Cook: 15 min. per batch   Other: 5 min.

1	cup all-purpose flour
½	tsp. baking soda
½	tsp. ground cinnamon
¼	tsp. salt
½	cup plus 2 Tbsp. unsalted butter, softened
½	cup granulated sugar
½	cup firmly packed light brown sugar
1	large egg
1	tsp. fiori di sicilia or orange extract (see note)
1	cup uncooked regular oats
8	oz. white chocolate, chopped (about 2 cups)
½	cup raisins or golden raisins

Combine first 4 ingredients in a medium bowl.

Beat butter at medium speed with an electric mixer until creamy; gradually add sugars, beating well. Beat in egg and orange flavoring just until combined. Add flour mixture and oats; stir until blended. Stir in white chocolate and raisins. Cover and chill dough 1 hour, if desired.

Line 2 large baking sheets with parchment paper. Drop batter by heaping tablespoonfuls, 3" apart, onto prepared baking sheets.

Bake at 350° for 13 to 15 minutes or until lightly browned. Cool on baking sheets 5 minutes. Transfer cookies to wire racks to cool completely. **Yield: about 2½ dozen.**

Note: Order fiori di sicilia from bakerscatalogue.com or call 800-827-6836. It's very affordable, and a small vial will perfume your kitchen for a long time.

gift idea • make ahead

Lemon-Coconut Snowballs

Lemon and coconut add a new twist to the traditional wedding cookie. Don't be shy when rolling these in powdered sugar—the more powdered sugar, the bigger the snowball!

Prep: 25 min.   Cook: 20 min. per batch   Other: 35 min.

1	cup unsalted butter, softened
½	cup powdered sugar
1	tsp. coconut extract
1	tsp. vanilla extract
2¼	cups all-purpose flour
1½	Tbsp. grated lemon rind
½	tsp. salt
1	cup sweetened flaked coconut, lightly toasted
1½	cups powdered sugar

Beat butter at medium speed with an electric mixer until creamy; gradually add ½ cup powdered sugar and extracts, beating well. Add flour, lemon rind, and salt, beating until combined. Stir in coconut. Cover and chill dough 30 minutes.

Shape dough into generous 1" balls; place 1" apart on parchment paper-lined baking sheets. Bake at 350° for 15 to 20 minutes or until golden on bottom, but pale on top. Transfer cookies to wire racks to cool 5 minutes.

Place 1½ cups powdered sugar in a bowl, and roll warm cookies in powdered sugar, coating well. Cool cookies completely on wire racks. Roll cooled cookies in powdered sugar again, coating well. **Yield: 2 dozen.**

Dark Chocolate-Espresso Shortbread

Cover dough portions with plastic wrap; gently press or roll each portion of dough into a 5½" circle. Lightly score each round with a sharp knife into 6 or 8 wedges.

Bake rounds at 325° for 23 minutes or until shortbread feels firm to the touch. Gently score each round again with a sharp knife. Slide parchment from baking sheets onto wire racks. Let shortbread cool completely on parchment. Cut shortbread into wedges along scored lines.

Melt chocolate baking bars separately in small bowls in the microwave according to package directions. Partially dip wide end of each shortbread wedge in unsweetened chocolate. Place on a wax paper-lined jelly-roll pan, and freeze briefly to set chocolate. Then partially dip other half of wide end of each wedge in white chocolate. Freeze briefly to set white chocolate. **Yield: 1½ to 2 dozen.**

gift idea
Pistachio-Cranberry Biscotti

Prep: 28 min.   Cook: 49 min.   Other: 10 min.

6	Tbsp. unsalted butter, softened
¾	cup sugar
2	large eggs
1	Tbsp. grated orange rind
1½	tsp. orange extract
2¼	cups all-purpose flour
1½	tsp. baking powder
½	tsp. salt
1	cup orange-flavored sweetened dried cranberries
¾	cup shelled natural salted pistachio nuts, chopped

Beat butter and sugar in a large bowl at medium speed with an electric mixer until light and fluffy. Add eggs, beating well; beat in orange rind and extract.

Combine flour, baking powder, and salt; add to butter mixture, beating at low speed until blended. Stir in cranberries and pistachios.

Divide dough in half. Using lightly floured hands, shape each portion into a 14" x 2" log. Place both logs 3" apart on a large baking sheet lined with parchment paper.

Bake at 325° for 28 minutes or until firm to the touch. Cool logs on baking sheet 10 minutes.

Cut each log into ½"-thick diagonal slices with a serrated knife using a gentle sawing motion. Place slices, cut side down, on baking sheet. Bake 9 minutes; turn cookies over, and bake 12 more minutes. Transfer biscotti to wire racks to cool completely. **Yield: 1½ dozen.**

editor's favorite • make ahead
Dark Chocolate-Espresso Shortbread

Edges tipped with unsweetened chocolate and white chocolate enhance the coffee flavor in these cookies.

Prep: 33 min.   Cook: 23 min.

1¼	cups all-purpose flour
¼	cup cornstarch
¼	cup unsweetened cocoa
1	tsp. instant espresso powder or instant coffee powder (we tested with Café Bustello)
¼	tsp. salt
1	cup unsalted butter, softened
1	cup powdered sugar
3	oz. white chocolate baking bar (we tested with Ghirardelli)
3	oz. unsweetened chocolate baking bars

Combine first 5 ingredients in a medium bowl; set aside.

Beat butter at medium speed with an electric mixer until fluffy; gradually add powdered sugar, beating well. Stir in dry ingredients; beat just until blended.

Line 2 baking sheets with parchment paper. Divide dough into 3 equal portions. Place 2 portions on opposite ends of 1 baking sheet. Place remaining portion on second baking sheet.

Peanut Butter Candy Bar Brownies

Peanut Butter Candy Bar Brownies

Peanut butter sandwich cookies become the crumb crust for these hunky bars loaded with chunks of candy bar.

Prep: 26 min. Cook: 35 min.

1   (16-oz.) package peanut-shaped peanut butter
    sandwich cookies, crushed
½   cup butter, melted
1   (14-oz.) can sweetened condensed milk
½   cup creamy peanut butter
1   Tbsp. vanilla extract
5   (1.5-oz.) packages chocolate-covered peanut butter
    cup candies, coarsely chopped
2   (2.1-oz.) chocolate-covered crispy peanut buttery
    candy bars, coarsely chopped (we tested with
    Butterfinger)
1   cup semisweet chocolate morsels
½   cup honey-roasted peanuts
½   cup sweetened flaked coconut

Combine crushed cookies and butter in a medium bowl. Press crumb mixture into bottom of a greased aluminum foil-lined 13" x 9" pan, allowing foil to extend over ends of pan. Bake at 350° for 6 to 8 minutes.

Combine condensed milk, peanut butter, and vanilla in a medium bowl, stirring until smooth.

Sprinkle chopped candy bars, chocolate morsels, peanuts, and coconut over crust. Drizzle condensed milk mixture over coconut.

Bake at 350° for 27 minutes or until lightly browned. Remove to a wire rack, and let cool in pan. Use foil to lift uncut brownies out of pan. Peel foil away from sides of uncut brownies, and cut into bars. **Yield: 28 small bars or 18 large bars.**

Pistachio-Cranberry Biscotti

Death by Caramel Bars

Add to butter mixture, stirring just until blended. Fold in chopped candy bars.

Spoon batter into a greased aluminum foil-lined 13" x 9" pan coated with cooking spray, allowing foil to extend over ends of pan. (Pan will be very full.) Spoon dollops of dulce de leche over batter; swirl slightly into batter with a knife. Bake at 325° for 1 hour and 5 minutes. Remove to a wire rack, and cool completely. (This may take several hours.) Use foil to lift uncut brownies out of pan. Peel foil away from sides of uncut brownies, and cut into bars. **Yield: 2 dozen.**

*Find dulce de leche with other Mexican ingredients or on the baking aisle.

editor's favorite
Mudslide Brownies

Yummy ingredients from the popular drink make a splash in these decadent bars.

Prep: 21 min.   Cook: 35 min.

6   (1-oz.) unsweetened chocolate baking squares
½   cup plus 2 Tbsp. unsalted butter, divided
1   cup granulated sugar
1   cup firmly packed light brown sugar
3   large eggs
4   tsp. espresso powder, divided (we tested with Café Bustello)
2   Tbsp. plus 2 tsp. coffee liqueur, divided
1½   cups all-purpose flour
½   tsp. salt
1   cup chopped pecans, toasted
2   Tbsp. whipping cream or half-and-half
2   Tbsp. vodka
2¼   to 2½ cups powdered sugar
Garnish: chocolate-covered espresso coffee beans, chopped

Melt 4 chocolate baking squares and ½ cup butter in a heavy saucepan over low heat, stirring occasionally. Remove from heat, and transfer to a large bowl. Add sugars; stir well. Stir in eggs, 2 tsp. espresso powder, and 2 tsp. coffee liqueur. Add flour and salt, stirring until blended. Stir in pecans.

Spread batter into a lightly greased aluminum foil-lined 13" x 9" pan (or see note on next page). Bake at 325° for 20 to 25 minutes or until brownies appear set on top. Cool completely in pan on a wire rack.

Melt remaining 2 chocolate baking squares and 2 Tbsp. butter in heavy saucepan, stirring occasionally. Remove

editor's favorite • make ahead
Death by Caramel Bars

These showy brownies are nice and tall with pockets of caramel goo. They are wicked enough on their own, but for an over-the-top dessert, add a scoop of vanilla ice cream and drizzle with caramel sauce.

Prep: 24 min.   Cook: 1 hr., 5 min.

3   cups firmly packed light brown sugar
2   cups unsalted butter, melted
3   large eggs, lightly beaten
1   Tbsp. vanilla extract
4   cups all-purpose flour
1   cup uncooked regular oats
1   tsp. baking powder
½   tsp. baking soda
¾   tsp. salt
6   (2.07-oz.) chocolate-coated caramel-peanut nougat bars, chopped (we tested with Snickers)
1   (14-oz.) can dulce de leche*

Combine first 4 ingredients in a large bowl; stir well. Combine flour, oats, baking powder, baking soda, and salt.

Mudslide Brownies

from heat; transfer to a medium bowl. Stir in remaining 2 tsp. espresso powder, whipping cream, vodka, and remaining 2 Tbsp. coffee liqueur. Add enough powdered sugar to make a good spreading consistency, beating at medium speed with an electric mixer until smooth. Spread frosting over cooled brownies; garnish, if desired. Let stand until frosting is set. Use foil to lift uncut brownies out of the pan. Cut into bars to serve. **Yield: 3 dozen small or 1 dozen large.**

Note: For really thick, showy brownies, we baked these in an 11" x 7½" pan at 325° for 26 to 28 minutes.

Entertaining

A remarkably easy Christmas feast, a lively Mexican fiesta,
a nifty party snacks swap, and an array of healthy menus
fill these pages. Over 50 recipes and decorating ideas
set your table with all you need for warm and
happy gatherings this holiday season.

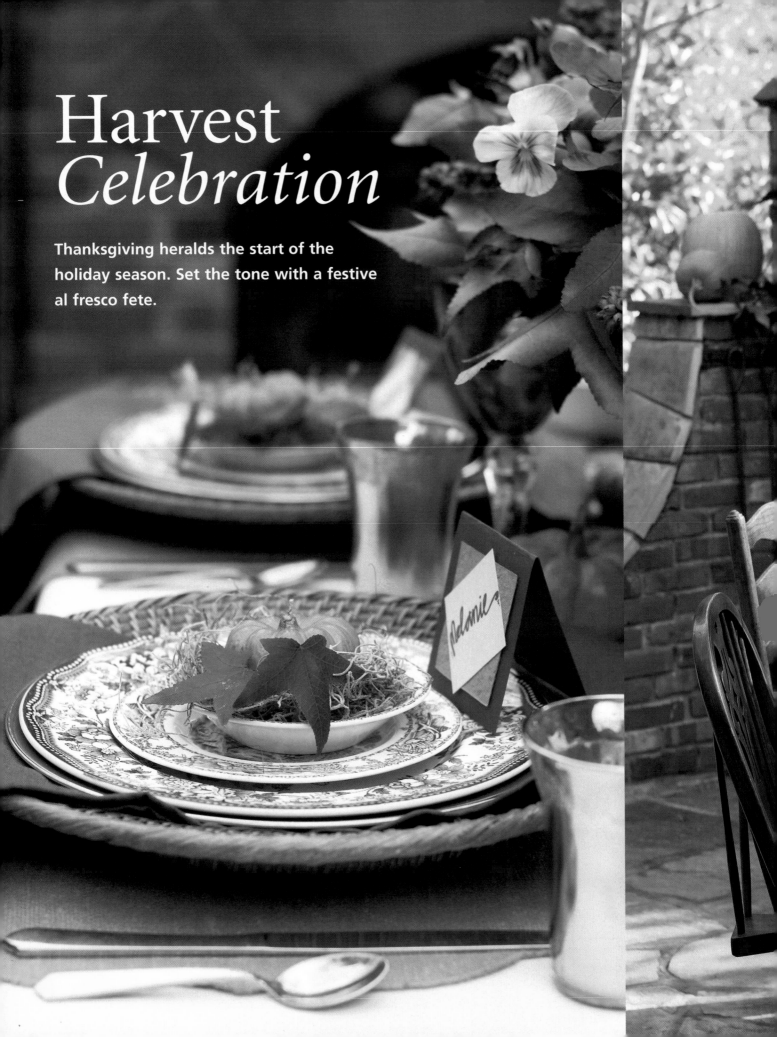

Harvest
Celebration

Thanksgiving heralds the start of the
holiday season. Set the tone with a festive
al fresco fete.

Golden Opportunity

Savor the season by setting your Thanksgiving feast outdoors. Colored leaves of rich golds and rusts provide autumnal ambience. Enhancing the scene is a plethora of pumpkins and table decorations in shades of mulberry and mauve.

Ornamental Orb

As the signature fruit of the season, pumpkins make a showstopping centerpiece. Fill a large container with moistened florist foam. Stack a large and a small pumpkin atop the foam. To secure the arrangement, insert a long florist pick into the top of the large pumpkin; then insert the pick into the bottom of the small pumpkin. Fill in around the pumpkins with a colorful mix of berries and leaves; insert stems lush with persimmons into the florist foam. Fit small pots of pansies between the florist foam and the sides of the container.

▲ Lay on the Charm

Embellish place settings to heighten the holiday attitude. Pair delicate dinnerware, such as this mulberry transferware, with woven chargers to harmonize with the casual outdoor surroundings. Add visual interest to the table by mixing and matching glasses, as evidenced here with a plum-colored goblet and a bronze tumbler. In lieu of traditional tapers, place pumpkin candles in saucers on the table to contribute a friendly glow. To fashion a place card, fold a rectangle of colored paper in half and glue on a square of paper in a contrasting color. Then write a guest's name on another paper square, and glue it to the card at an angle.

◀ Clever Presentation

Instead of using a conventional tray, pull out a pretty platter to hold such items as cups and saucers for after-dinner coffee or dessert plates and forks.

Gather Together

Pumpkin candles in various sizes grace this mantel, echoing autumn's splendor.
If you don't have an outdoor mantel, use this setup on a side table or in a more
diminutive form on the dining table. For the center of the arrangement, fill a
container, such as a tureen, with small pots of pansies and leaves. Place pumpkin
candles or small pumpkins on each side of the container, and link the individual
elements by punctuating them with leaves, small berries, or rose hips.

From Everyday
to Holiday

Get your everyday table setting holiday
ready with just a few quick adjustments. These
photos show you how it's done.

Quick Change

Candleholders sporting pears and a wooden compote filled with fresh fruits form
an easy centerpiece that's both beautiful and functional for everyday. Two table
runners—placed across the table rather than lengthwise—stand in for separate
place mats. White plates, clear glassware, and wooden-handle utensils are basic
tableware (above). With these essentials in place, your table is set for a speedy
makeover that will make it ready for a holiday party in no time flat (right). See
Stylish Substitutions on page 106 for all the details.

Stylish Substitutions

It's easy to make the switch from everyday to holiday with just a few key substitutions. Here's how:

Everyday Table	Holiday Table
• White dinner plates	• Add cream-colored chargers. • Add mocha-colored salad plates. • Add pinecone candles and greenery and berry clippings in a small bowl. Let each guest take home a candle as a memento.
• White napkins	• Substitute with red napkins.
• Clear glassware	• Substitute with red water and wine goblets.
• Fruit on compote	• Substitute with miniature Christmassy chapel surrounded with pine and berry clippings.
• Pears on candleholders	• Substitute with twig trees topped with bows.

Holiday extras:
Add fresh clippings, tiny pinecones, and ornaments around the base of the compote and candleholders. Finish the look with additional twig trees and red pillar candles.

Cup of Cheer

At each place setting, fill a small cup or bowl with a decorative candle (left), which doubles as a mood-setting detail and take-home party favor. Tuck in short stems of pine and berries to keep the candle company. Then knot brown satin ribbon around a fanned-out napkin for a rich contrast of colors and textures (above).

Final Detail ▶

Complete the seasonal transition with a charming chair decoration. Tie a twig star to the chair back with brown ribbon layered atop a wider red ribbon to repeat colors from the table setting.

Tradition
with a Twist

Introduce unexpected accessories to the holiday table for a fresh look that's definitely not the standard bill of fare.

Showcase the Centerpiece

Consider using a glass terrarium as a centerpiece that's beautifully fresh all season long. Not only will this display last longer than a floral arrangement, but it will also bestow elegant sophistication to the entire room. Plant lacy ferns in the bottom of the terrarium; or tuck in small containers of ferns, and hide the pots with moss. Place a tall Christmassy accent piece, such as a mercury glass tree, in the center of the terrarium. Add similar accents or tall pillar candles on each side of the piece. Soften the edges of the arrangement with bits of evergreen.

A Sparkling Setting

Select table decorations with reflective surfaces to set a refined table that is richly understated yet no less festive. Here, mercury glass trees and votive holders amidst circles of beaded garlands catch the twinkle of lights from the tree.

Add small details to the luxury of the setting. Layer a crochet-edged table runner atop a linen tablecloth, and use trimmed napkins in a soft shade of mauve as delicate complements. Choose mauve-colored glasses to enhance the color scheme.

⊿ Warm Glow

Place a candle at each seat for a welcome that shines with the warmth of the holiday spirit. Encircle the votive holder with a wintry glass garland to reflect the candle's light. When dinner is served, guests can set their candles aside to be carried home later as glowing reminders of a lovely evening shared with friends.

Fast Fix ▶

Filling a decorative container with beautiful ornaments is one of the quickest ways to impart a seasonal accent to a room. Search out unusual pieces, such as this small terrarium, to boost the appeal of the arrangement.

A Sterling Idea

Present flatware in stocking-shaped ornaments for a darling detail that will have everyone abuzz. This presentation works especially well at a buffet, since guests can easily collect their flatware while also holding their plates. Write the year and event on the back of each stocking for personalized favors.

Lighten Up

Send dark Christmas crimsons and greens on holiday, and rely instead on bright red accents paired with chartreuse for a simplified setting.

Ever Green

From lemon-leaf wreaths basking in the sunlight to wide ribbon simply tied to each chair, chartreuse exudes chic style in this modern holiday setting. Against a neutral background, this cool shade makes reds appear even more vivid.

Gather pale green and red amaryllis blooms to create an aromatic place card. The wide array of colors offered by this flower can pull together any nontraditional Christmas color scheme. For a favor each guest can enjoy at home, arrange the trumpet-shaped blooms in a bouquet tied with matching ribbon before placing them in a mug.

Instant Success

Far from austere, these spiky holly boughs need no embellishment to achieve maximum results. Fill clear glass vases with a couple of inches of water, and then add holly stems—it's that simple. Placing the stems at angles in the vases fashions a bold, three-dimensional focal point that spreads its charm beyond the table to the entire room.

Naturally *Casual*

Let Mother Nature do the decorating with pots of fresh greenery. Accessorize the color scheme with playful accents, such as gift boxes, ornaments, fruits, and votive candles.

Heightened Impact

To make the most of this centerpiece, set it on a slightly elevated surface, such as the miniature sleigh pictured here. Be sure the centerpiece is low enough that guests can view each other across the table. Place a potted evergreen in a brightly colored pot, and cover the potting soil with red-hued apples and sprigs of pine. Use an unexpected accent, such as the chalkboard star, to introduce a touch of whimsy.

At place settings, pair sparkling red with zesty lime. Top each plate with a votive holder filled with kosher salt, a sprig of greenery, and a tiny pinecone; then tuck in a personalized place card made from a gift tag decorated with ribbon and stickers.

Plant small pots of ryegrass to dot around the table, mantel, or wherever you'd like a hint of the outdoors. Dress up each pot by gluing a strip of decorative ribbon around the rim. (See the box below for growing directions for ryegrass.)

How to Grow Ryegrass

It takes 18 to 20 days for ryegrass to grow, so plan accordingly in order to include it in your holiday decorations.

1. Gather the supplies (available at garden centers): 3- to 4-inch shallow containers or pots with drainage holes; potting soil; ryegrass seed; spray bottle filled with water.

2. Fill each container about halfway with soil.

3. Sprinkle a solid layer of seeds on the soil, but don't pile them on top of each other. Rake the seeds lightly with a fork until they are covered with soil.

4. Spray lightly to moisten the soil. Place the containers in a well-lit area; keep the soil moist by spraying it a couple of times daily until the seeds sprout (in about 10 days). Continue to spray the grass daily.

5. Use scissors to "mow" the grass as needed when it reaches the desired height. The potted grass will stay green for up to 3 weeks.

Dressed for Dinner

A few snips of ribbon transform plain napkins into showy table accessories that are striking yet simple.

Terrific Tie-Ups

For a winning combination, pair two trims, such as the rick-rack and curly ribbon shown on the opposite page. (Clockwise from top, left) Add sparkle to a neutral place setting with shimmery ribbon; for a sweet finish, tie chocolates to the ribbon tails. Give red plates a sophisticated complement with decorative brown ribbon; here, a traditional bow ties a napkin into a neat package. Crisscross grosgrain ribbon around a napkin, and finish with a tiny treasure for a casual look that blends perfectly with a pottery plate. For a fancy touch, knot dramatic ribbon around each napkin.

Christmas Dinner: Grand Style Made Easy

Host the holiday get-together with ease. Let our Foods staff walk you through the planning, from turkey basics to setting a pretty table. This classic Southern feast features both ham and turkey options, side dishes with make-ahead tips, and a simple fruit dessert as well as a luscious cake.

Honey and Brown Sugar-Crusted Ham or
Marmalade-Glazed Turkey and Giblet Gravy

Shortcut Cornbread Dressing • Cranberry-Maple Sauce

Citrus Sweet Potato Rounds • Succotash • Seasoned Green Beans

Waldorf Salad Jubilee

Bakery dinner rolls

Spiced Ambrosia or

Pumpkin-Rum Cake with Brown Sugar Icing

Wine or Iced tea

menu for 10

game plan

Before the Day

As much as 3 months ahead:

• Purchase ingredients for Shortcut Cornbread Dressing; prepare, cover, and freeze it unbaked (or prepare dressing 1 day ahead and refrigerate).

2 weeks ahead:

• Make grocery list. Shop for nonperishables.
• Plan table centerpiece and/or decorations.

3 or 4 days ahead:

• Do remaining shopping.
• Place turkey in refrigerator to thaw, if frozen.

2 days ahead:

• Set table and organize serving pieces.
• Arrange table centerpiece.
• Toast pecans for Waldorf Salad Jubilee; store in a zip-top plastic bag.
• Hard-cook egg for Giblet Gravy. Store in refrigerator.
• Chop onion and celery for Giblet Gravy, Shortcut Cornbread Dressing, and Waldorf Salad Jubilee; label and store in airtight plastic bags. Or buy prechopped onion and celery.
• Prepare Cranberry-Maple Sauce; cover and refrigerate.
• Cook sweet potatoes for Citrus Sweet Potato Rounds; let cool, and refrigerate overnight.

1 day ahead:

• Thaw frozen Shortcut Cornbread Dressing in refrigerator, or prepare dressing, cover, and refrigerate.
• Bake Pumpkin-Rum Cake.
• Slice potatoes and prepare recipe for Citrus Sweet Potato Rounds; cover and chill.
• Cook green beans; store in zip-top plastic bag in refrigerator.
• Combine apple mixture for Waldorf Salad Jubilee; cover and chill. Wash radicchio for salad; place in plastic bag, and refrigerate.
• Prepare fruit and syrup for Spiced Ambrosia; cover and chill in separate containers.
• Brew tea, if desired.

The Day of

5 hours ahead:

• Review plan for the day, and get organized.
• Ready ham for baking; cover loosely, and refrigerate.

3 hours ahead:

• Prepare turkey, and bake; then cover with aluminum foil.
• Let ham come to room temperature.

2 hours ahead:

• Bake ham; then cover with aluminum foil.
• Simmer broth for Giblet Gravy.
• Let Shortcut Cornbread Dressing come to room temperature.

1 hour ahead:

• Prepare Succotash; hold out bacon, tomatoes, and seasonings.

• Let Citrus Sweet Potato Rounds stand at room temperature.
• Bake Shortcut Cornbread Dressing.

30 minutes ahead:

• Bake Citrus Sweet Potato Rounds.
• Finish preparing Seasoned Green Beans and Giblet Gravy.

10 minutes ahead:

• Heat rolls.
• Add pecans to Waldorf Salad Jubilee; serve in radicchio leaves.
• Heat Succotash; stir in bacon, tomatoes, basil, salt, and pepper.

After dinner:

• Have dessert plates ready for Pumpkin-Rum Cake.
• Serve ambrosia in stemless tumblers; sprinkle with coconut.

Apple and Calla Lily Centerpiece

▲ Core apples with an apple corer.

▲ Trim calla lilies and insert one into each cored apple. Add seeded eucalyptus.

◄ Insert a candle into center of each calla lily, and build a centerpiece around apples. We filled stemless wine tumblers with a little water, and added fresh cranberries and calla lilies.

Place cards

◄ Tie small name cards around stems of wine glasses using ribbon or tuck name cards into calla lily apples as another option (below).

Honey and Brown Sugar-Crusted Ham

A dark brown sugar crust makes this ham incredibly yummy. Any leftover slices should make their way onto biscuits.

Prep: 6 min.   Cook: 2 hr., 15 min.   Other: 15 min.

1   (9- to 10-lb.) ready-to-cook, bone-in ham shank
¾   cup honey
1   cup firmly packed dark brown sugar
1   tsp. ground nutmeg
1   tsp. ground cinnamon
1   tsp. ground cloves

▲ Brush honey on partially baked ham. It serves as the "glue" for the brown sugar crust.

▲ Pat sugar and spice coating onto honeyed ham.

Ham ready for final baking

Slice away hard outer skin from ham with a sharp knife, leaving a thin layer of fat. Place ham, fat side up, on a rack in a shallow roasting pan. Score top of ham in a diamond pattern; insert a meat thermometer into ham, making sure it does not touch fat or bone.

Bake ham on lowest oven rack at 325° for 1½ hours. Remove ham from oven, leaving oven on. Brush ham with honey. Combine sugar and spices; pat over honey, coating ham well.

Return ham to oven, and continue to bake at 325° for 35 to 45 minutes or until thermometer registers 148°. (Cover ham with aluminum foil during the last 20 minutes, if necessary, to prevent excessive browning.) Let ham stand 15 minutes before carving. **Yield: 10 servings.**

Marmalade-Glazed Turkey and Giblet Gravy

Juicy meat and darkly glazed skin set this holiday bird apart. A wonderful orange marmalade and honey glaze gives this a sweet twist from grandma's traditional turkey. If your turkey is frozen, place turkey in its original wrapper in a pan, and refrigerate two to three days or until thawed.

Prep: 8 min.   Cook: 3 hr.   Other: 15 min.

1   (10- to 12-lb.) fresh or frozen turkey, thawed
1½   tsp. salt
1   tsp. pepper
1   tsp. dried whole savory, crumbled
1   tsp. rubbed sage
¼   cup unsalted butter, softened
½   cup orange juice
½   cup orange marmalade
1   Tbsp. honey
Garnishes: oranges, fresh sage
Giblet Gravy (opposite)

Remove giblets and neck from turkey; place in refrigerator for use in Giblet Gravy. Rinse turkey with cold water; pat dry with paper towels. Place turkey, breast side up, on a rack in a lightly greased roasting pan. Lift wing tips up and over back, and tuck under bird.

Combine salt and next 3 ingredients in a small bowl; rub some of seasoning inside turkey cavity. Combine remaining herb mixture with softened butter, and rub all over outside of turkey, legs and all. Tie ends of legs together with heavy string or tuck under flap of skin around tail.

Bake, uncovered, at 325° for 1 hour and 30 minutes.

Combine orange juice, marmalade, and honey, stirring well. Brush half of orange glaze over turkey; bake 1 to 1½ hours or until a meat thermometer inserted into meaty part of thigh registers 170°, brushing with orange glaze every 30 minutes. Shield turkey with aluminum foil during cooking, if necessary, to prevent overbrowning.

Transfer turkey to a serving platter, reserving pan drippings for Giblet Gravy. Let turkey stand, covered with foil, 15 minutes before carving. Garnish platter, if desired. Serve turkey with Giblet Gravy. **Yield: 10 to 12 servings.**

Giblet Gravy

Prep: 5 min.   Cook: 1 hr., 51 min.

Giblets and neck reserved from turkey
4   cups water
Pan drippings from roasted turkey
1   small onion, chopped
1   celery rib, chopped
1   tsp. salt
½   tsp. pepper
2   Tbsp. cornstarch
¼   cup water
1   hard-cooked large egg, chopped
Salt and pepper to taste

Combine giblets, neck, and water in a saucepan. Bring to a boil; cover, reduce heat, and simmer 1 hour or until giblets are tender. Strain, reserving broth. Discard turkey neck. Coarsely chop giblets; set aside.

Skim and discard fat from reserved pan drippings of roasted turkey. Add reserved broth (at least 2½ cups) to pan drippings; stir until browned bits are loosened from bottom of roasting pan.

Transfer broth and drippings to a saucepan, if desired, or continue cooking in roasting pan over 2 burners on the stove. Stir in chopped giblets. Add onion and next 3 ingredients. Bring to a boil; reduce heat, and simmer, uncovered, 30 minutes.

Combine cornstarch and ¼ cup water, stirring well; gradually stir into gravy. Bring to a boil; boil 1 minute or until thickened. Stir in egg. Add salt and pepper to taste. Serve hot. **Yield: 4 cups.**

Turkey Talk

In 2006 the USDA determined a new minimum doneness temperature of 165° for both white and dark meat poultry; however, this minimum internal temperature for food safety may not achieve the desired doneness for personal preferences and best quality. For this recipe, the turkey was best when baked to a slightly higher temperature of 170° that our taste panel preferred. And we recommend buying a fresh bird. If you buy a frozen bird, be sure it is completely thawed—especially in the center. Check it after you remove the giblets. Otherwise, the turkey may need to cook a bit longer to reach proper doneness.

▲ Lift wing tips up and over back, and tuck under bird.

▲ Rub herb butter all over bird.

▲ Brush some of orange marmalade glaze over partially roasted turkey.

▲ Insert a thermometer into the meaty part of the thigh in search of 170° ideal doneness for this recipe.

▲ Using packaged cornbread and refrigerated biscuits shaves time off preparing this dressing. Look for prechopped onion and celery in the produce section of the grocery store.

make ahead
Shortcut Cornbread Dressing

Prep: 26 min.   Cook: 1 hr.

2	(6-oz.) packages cornbread mix (we tested with Martha White)
1	(6-oz.) can refrigerated buttermilk biscuits
¼	cup butter or margarine
1	large onion, chopped (2 cups)
5	celery ribs, chopped (1½ cups)
5	cups chicken broth
4	large eggs, lightly beaten
2	tsp. rubbed sage
1½	tsp. pepper
¾	tsp. salt

Prepare cornbread mix and biscuits according to package directions; let cool. Crumble cornbread and biscuits in a large bowl. Set aside.

Melt butter in a large skillet over medium-high heat; add onion and celery, and sauté until tender. Add sautéed vegetables, broth, and remaining ingredients to crumbled cornbread; stir well. Spoon dressing into a lightly greased 13" x 9" baking dish.

Bake, uncovered, at 350° for 55 minutes or until browned. **Yield: 10 servings.**

Make-Ahead Note: Prepare recipe as directed; do not bake. Cover and freeze dressing up to 3 months or refrigerate up to 24 hours. Remove from refrigerator; let stand 30 minutes. Uncover and bake as directed.

gift idea • make ahead • quick & easy
Cranberry-Maple Sauce

Aside from its traditional place on the holiday dinner plate, this sauce makes a great topping for waffles or pancakes, too.

Prep: 5 min.   Cook: 12 min.

1	(12-oz.) package fresh or frozen cranberries (3 cups)
¾	cup pure maple syrup (not pancake syrup)
½	cup firmly packed light brown sugar
¼	cup water
½	tsp. vanilla extract

Combine all ingredients in a heavy saucepan. Bring mixture to a boil; reduce heat, and simmer 8 minutes or just until cranberries begin to pop, stirring often. Pour sauce into a serving bowl, and let cool completely. Serve chilled, if desired. **Yield: 2½ cups.**

Make-Ahead Note: Sauce can be made up to 1 week ahead. Keep covered in refrigerator.

▲ Simmer just until cranberries start to pop. The sauce will thicken as it cools.

▲ Spoon orange glaze over sweet potatoes before baking. The glaze thickens in the oven and coats the sweet potatoes.

make ahead

Citrus Sweet Potato Rounds

Vanilla bean paste enhances the glaze for these sweet potatoes.

Prep: 13 min.   Cook: 1 hr., 30 min.

7	medium sweet potatoes (about 4 lb.)
½	cup pecan halves
1	cup orange juice
⅔	cup firmly packed brown sugar
¼	cup butter, melted
1	Tbsp. cornstarch
¼	tsp. salt
1	tsp. vanilla bean paste or vanilla extract

Place washed sweet potatoes on a baking sheet; prick each potato with a fork. Bake at 450° for 45 minutes or until almost tender. Let potatoes cool to the touch.

Peel potatoes, and cut into ½"-thick slices. Arrange potato slices in a lightly greased 13" x 9" baking dish or round 3-qt. casserole. Top with pecan halves.

Combine orange juice and next 4 ingredients in a small saucepan, stirring well. Bring glaze mixture to a boil; boil 1 minute or until thickened and bubbly. Stir in vanilla bean paste. Pour or spoon orange glaze over sweet potato slices.

Bake, uncovered, at 350° for 30 to 45 minutes or until glaze is thickened. **Yield: 10 servings.**

Make-Ahead Note: After baked sweet potatoes have cooled, cover and refrigerate up to 24 hours. The next day, peel and slice potatoes, and let come to room temperature before baking as directed above.

make ahead • quick & easy

Succotash

We especially liked this side dish paired with ham.

Prep: 6 min.   Cook: 19 min.

5	bacon slices, coarsely chopped
2	green onions, chopped
4	cups frozen whole kernel corn, thawed
3½	cups frozen baby lima beans, thawed
¾	cup chicken broth
1	pt. grape tomatoes, halved
2	tsp. chopped fresh basil or ¾ tsp. dried basil
½	tsp. salt
½	tsp. pepper

Cook bacon in a large skillet until crisp; remove bacon, and drain on paper towels, reserving 3 tablespoons drippings in skillet.

Sauté green onions in hot drippings 2 minutes. Stir in corn, lima beans, and broth. Cook, uncovered, 15 minutes or until beans are just tender and most of broth evaporates, stirring often. Stir in bacon, tomatoes, basil, salt, and pepper. Cook 1 to 2 minutes or until thoroughly heated. **Yield: 10 servings.**

▲ Have tomatoes prepped and ready to add to Succotash just before serving.

Seasoned Green Beans

Every busy holiday menu needs at least one easy side dish.
Cook the beans and slice the onion a day ahead.

Prep: 13 min. Cook: 30 min.

2½ lb. green beans, trimmed
2   Tbsp. olive oil
1   onion, vertically sliced
4   garlic cloves, minced
1   tsp. salt
½   tsp. pepper

Cook green beans in boiling salted water 5 to 7 minutes
or until crisp-tender. Plunge beans in ice water to stop the
cooking process; drain and set aside.

Heat oil in a large skillet or sauté pan over medium heat;
add onion and garlic, and sauté 15 to 20 minutes or until
tender and onion starts to caramelize. Stir in green beans,
salt, and pepper; sauté 2 to 3 minutes or until beans are
heated. Serve hot. **Yield: 10 servings.**

Make-Ahead Note: Place cooked green beans in a large
zip-top plastic bag, and store in refrigerator up to 1 day.
When ready to use, simply toss in with caramelized
onions, and sauté until warm.

▲ Plunge crisp-tender beans in ice water to stop the cooking process.
Seal beans in a zip-top bag and refrigerate for make-ahead ease.

Waldorf Salad Jubilee

make ahead • quick & easy

Waldorf Salad Jubilee

This vibrant salad will brighten your holiday table. For a
slightly sweeter salad, use Gala or Fuji apples in place of
Granny Smith.

Prep: 26 min.

1   cup mayonnaise
1   tsp. lemon juice
½   tsp. salt
6   Granny Smith apples (about 2½ lb.), unpeeled and
     cut into ½" pieces
1½   cups chopped celery
1½   cups chopped radishes
¾   cup orange-flavored dried cranberries
½   cup finely chopped red onion
1½   cups pecan pieces, toasted
2   heads radicchio, washed, and leaves separated

Combine first 3 ingredients in a medium bowl, stirring
well. Toss apples with next 4 ingredients in a large bowl.
Add mayonnaise dressing, and toss to coat. (Salad can be
prepared a day ahead; cover and refrigerate overnight).

Fold toasted pecans into salad. Line a serving bowl with
radicchio leaves and spoon in salad or arrange radicchio
leaves on each plate, and spoon salad into leaves. **Yield:**
10 servings.

Spiced Ambrosia

Prep: 37 min.   Cook: 4 min.   Other: 8 hr.

½ cup water
½ cup sugar
1 (1" to 2") piece fresh ginger, peeled and thinly sliced
1 Tbsp. grated orange rind
1 (3") cinnamon stick
3 black peppercorns
½ tsp. vanilla extract
10 navel oranges, peeled and sectioned
1 (8-oz.) can pineapple tidbits in juice
¾ cup sweetened flaked coconut
¼ cup maraschino cherries with stems

Bring first 6 ingredients to a boil in a small saucepan over medium heat. Remove from heat; stir in vanilla.

Cover and let stand 30 minutes. Pour syrup through a wire-mesh strainer into a small bowl, discarding ginger and spices. Cool completely; chill.

Combine sectioned oranges and pineapple in a large bowl. Gently stir in chilled syrup. Spoon fruit and syrup into individual dessert dishes. Sprinkle with coconut, and top with cherries. **Yield: 10 servings.**

Make-Ahead Note: Prepare fruit. Seal in a zip-top freezer bag, and refrigerate overnight. Cover and chill ginger syrup overnight. Combine fruit and syrup before serving.

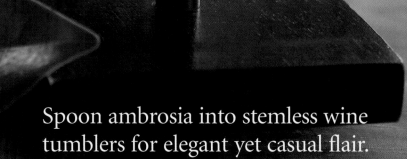

Spoon ambrosia into stemless wine tumblers for elegant yet casual flair.

Pumpkin-Rum Cake with
Brown Sugar Icing

Pumpkin-Rum Cake with Brown Sugar Icing

Pumpkin, a classic holiday flavor, gets blended with a yummy pecan streusel and doused with a fudgelike icing.

Prep: 21 min.   Cook: 1 hr., 28 min.   Other: 10 min.

¾   cup chopped pecans, toasted
¾   cup firmly packed dark brown sugar
3   Tbsp. all-purpose flour
1½ tsp. ground cinnamon
¼   cup butter, melted
1   cup unsalted butter, softened
2   cups granulated sugar
2   cups firmly packed dark brown sugar
5   large eggs
2   cups canned unsweetened pumpkin
¼   cup dark rum
3   cups all-purpose flour
2   tsp. baking powder
½   tsp. baking soda
¾   tsp. salt
2   tsp. ground cinnamon
½   tsp. ground ginger
½   tsp. ground allspice
½   tsp. ground nutmeg
¾   cup firmly packed dark brown sugar
½   cup whipping cream
¼   cup unsalted butter
1   tsp. dark rum
1   cup plus 2 Tbsp. sifted powdered sugar

Combine first 4 ingredients in a small bowl; stir in ¼ cup melted butter. Use fingers to pinch streusel into big clumps. Set aside.

Beat 1 cup butter at medium speed with an electric mixer about 2 minutes or until creamy. Gradually add 2 cups each granulated and dark brown sugar, beating at medium speed 5 to 7 minutes. Add eggs, 1 at a time, beating just until yellow disappears.

Stir together pumpkin and ¼ cup rum in a bowl. Combine flour and next 7 ingredients in a medium bowl. Add flour mixture to butter mixture alternately with pumpkin, beginning and ending with flour.

Pour half of batter into a well-greased and floured 12-cup Bundt pan. (We recommend greasing pan with shortening.) Sprinkle batter with streusel; top with remaining batter.

Bake at 325° for 1 hour and 28 minutes or until a long wooden pick inserted in center comes out clean. Cool in

A splash of dark rum enhances both this dreamy icing and moist cake.

pan on a wire rack 10 minutes; remove from pan, and let cool completely.

Combine ¾ cup brown sugar, whipping cream, and ¼ cup unsalted butter in a medium saucepan. Cook, stirring constantly, over medium-low heat, until butter melts and sugar dissolves. Increase heat to medium-high, and bring to a boil. Boil 3 minutes. Remove from heat, and stir in 1 tsp. rum.

Place powdered sugar in a bowl; pour brown sugar mixture over powdered sugar, stirring with a wire whisk 1 minute or until smooth. Let cool 20 to 25 minutes or until lukewarm. Spoon icing over cooled cake, and let stand until icing is firm. **Yield: 12 servings.**

Christmas Party
in the Kitchen

Many parties end up in the kitchen, so go ahead and declare it party headquarters. Make it a casual holiday get-together and involve your friends in the cooking.

Open-Faced Chile-Cheese Quesadillas

Roasted Tomato Salsa • Orange, Red Onion, and Mint Salad

Steak Fajitas with Sautéed Onions and Peppers

Mexican Rice and Cheese Casserole

Deep, Rich Mexican Hot Chocolate • Chipotle-Chocolate Toffee (page 158)

menu for 10

game plan

1 day ahead:
- Prepare Roasted Tomato Salsa.
- Marinate beef.
- Assemble Mexican Rice and Cheese Casserole; refrigerate.
- Prepare Chipotle-Chocolate Toffee (page 158), if serving.

1 to 4 hours ahead:
- Prepare ingredients and dressing for salad; chill separately.

1 hour ahead:
- Sauté onions and peppers for fajitas, and keep warm.

½ hour ahead:
- Bake Mexican Rice and Cheese Casserole.

Last minute:
- Get everybody working on quesadillas.
- Grill steak, and slice.
- Dress salad.

Just after dinner:
- Prepare dessert drinks.

quick & easy

Open-Faced Chile-Cheese Quesadillas

These quesadillas make easy party hors d'oeuvres. The topping can be prepared a day ahead and kept covered in the refrigerator. The flour tortillas can be baked several hours ahead and kept at room temperature until ready to top. Let your guests help top the tortillas before baking and cut them up for serving.

Prep: 7 min.   Cook: 14 min.

5	(8") flour tortillas
	Olive oil
2	cups (8 oz.) shredded Monterey Jack cheese with peppers or Monterey Jack cheese
½	cup bottled roasted red bell peppers, drained and finely chopped
½	cup pitted ripe olives, drained and chopped
1	to 2 chipotle chiles in adobo sauce, chopped
1	tsp. adobo sauce
¼	cup minced fresh cilantro

Open-Faced Chile-Cheese Quesadillas,
Roasted Tomato Salsa

Brush tortillas lightly with olive oil; prick each tortilla several times with a fork. Place tortillas on 2 large baking sheets. Bake at 400° for 6 minutes or until lightly browned and puffed. Let tortillas cool before topping.

Combine cheese and next 5 ingredients. Sprinkle cheese mixture evenly over tortillas.

Bake at 400° for 6 to 8 minutes or until cheese melts. Cut each tortilla into 6 wedges; arrange wedges on a serving platter. **Yield: 30 appetizer servings.**

make ahead
Roasted Tomato Salsa

Roasting the tomatoes and vegetables for this salsa gives it a wonderful depth of flavor. Unlike fresh tomato salsas, which are generally eaten soon after preparation, this salsa can be prepared several days ahead.

Prep: 18 min.   Cook: 28 min.   Other: 10 min.

2   lb. plum tomatoes
2   to 3 large jalapeño peppers
1   small onion, sliced
6   garlic cloves, peeled
1   Tbsp. olive oil
¼   cup tomato juice
¼   cup minced fresh cilantro
1   tsp. salt
2   tsp. cider vinegar

Arrange tomatoes and jalapeños on a lightly greased baking sheet; broil 5½" from heat 10 to 15 minutes or until lightly charred and blistered, turning once or twice. Transfer jalapeños to a bowl, and let cool. Place tomatoes in a large zip-top plastic bag; seal and let stand 10 minutes.

Combine onion, garlic, and olive oil in a bowl; transfer to a baking sheet. Bake at 450° for 10 minutes, stirring once, until golden and soft.

Remove stems from jalapeños, and transfer whole peppers to a food processor. Add onion and garlic; process until finely chopped, scraping down sides of bowl. Transfer mixture to a bowl.

Peel tomatoes over a bowl to catch juices. (Do not seed.) Transfer peeled tomatoes to food processor; process until coarsely chopped. Add to jalapeño mixture, stirring well. Stir in tomato juice and remaining ingredients. Store in an airtight container in refrigerator up to 2 days. Serve salsa at room temperature. **Yield: 3¾ cups.**

Orange, Red Onion, and Mint Salad

make ahead • quick & easy
Orange, Red Onion, and Mint Salad

Prepare and chill this colorful salad up to three hours ahead. Lightly dress and toss greens right before serving. Use Valencia oranges; they're both sweet and tart with an intense citrus flavor.

Prep: 16 min.

2   heads romaine lettuce, chopped
5   Valencia or navel oranges, peeled and sectioned or sliced
1   small red onion, thinly sliced, separated into rings, and halved
2   avocados, sliced
2   Tbsp. lime juice
1   Tbsp. white or red wine vinegar
½   tsp. salt
½   tsp. ground cumin
¼   tsp. freshly ground black pepper
Pinch of sugar
⅓   cup olive oil
3   Tbsp. minced fresh mint
8   fresh mint leaves

Combine first 4 ingredients in a salad bowl.

Combine lime juice and next 5 ingredients in a small bowl; slowly add oil in a thin stream, whisking constantly. Drizzle dressing over salad; sprinkle with minced mint, and toss. Top with mint leaves. **Yield: 10 servings.**

Steak Fajitas with Sautéed Onions and Peppers

Skirt steak is the traditional cut used to make beef fajitas. Aside from being full of flavor, it's a relatively inexpensive cut of meat, perfect for large gatherings. Marinating the steak overnight only improves its flavor and tenderness.

Prep: 27 min.   Cook: 25 min.   Other: 8 hr.

½ cup olive oil
12 garlic cloves, minced
¼ cup lime juice
4 tsp. ground cumin
1 tsp. salt
½ tsp. freshly ground black pepper
3 lb. skirt steak or flank steak
3 Tbsp. olive oil
1 large red bell pepper, cut lengthwise into ½" strips
1 large yellow bell pepper, cut lengthwise into ½" strips
1 large orange bell pepper, cut lengthwise into ½" strips
2 large onions, sliced and separated into rings
1½ tsp. dried oregano
4 garlic cloves, minced
¼ cup minced fresh cilantro
10 (10") flour tortillas
Toppings: Roasted Tomato Salsa, guacamole, sour cream

Combine first 6 ingredients in a shallow dish. Add steak, turning to coat with marinade. Cover and chill 8 hours.

Heat 3 Tbsp. oil in a large cast-iron skillet over medium-high heat. Add bell peppers, onions, and oregano. Cook 12 minutes or until tender, stirring often. Add

▲ Thinly slice grilled steak for serving.

remaining minced garlic, and cook 2 minutes, stirring often. Stir in cilantro. Keep warm.

Warm tortillas according to package directions.

Remove steak from marinade, discarding marinade. Grill steak, covered with grill lid, over medium-high heat (350° to 400°) 5 minutes on each side or to desired degree of doneness. Transfer steak to a cutting board, and let stand 10 minutes. Cut steak diagonally across the grain into thin strips. Serve with tortillas, onions and peppers, and desired toppings. **Yield: 10 servings.**

Mexican Rice and Cheese Casserole

Prep: 12 min.   Cook: 45 min.

2 (8-oz.) packages Mexican Rice (we tested with Vigo)
2 cups (8 oz.) shredded Monterey Jack cheese, divided
1 cup thinly sliced green onions
1 (8-oz.) container sour cream
1 tsp. salt
¼ tsp. ground red pepper
¼ tsp. smoked or sweet paprika

Prepare rice according to package directions.

Combine hot cooked rice, 1½ cups shredded cheese, and next 4 ingredients in a large bowl; stir until combined.

Transfer seasoned rice mixture to a greased 13" x 9" baking dish; sprinkle with remaining ½ cup cheese and paprika.

Bake, uncovered, at 350° for 25 to 30 minutes or until thoroughly heated. **Yield: 10 servings.**

Deep, Rich Mexican Hot Chocolate

For a special touch, add a split vanilla bean to each mug as a stirrer stick—vanilla "seeds" will permeate the hot chocolate as you stir. (pictured on page 130)

Prep: 6 min.   Cook: 10 min.

9 cups milk
½ cup firmly packed dark brown sugar
2 (3.5-oz.) bars bittersweet chocolate, finely chopped
⅓ cup Dutch process or unsweetened cocoa
3 Tbsp. instant espresso powder
1½ tsp. ground cinnamon
⅔ cup coffee liqueur (optional)
Garnishes: sweetened whipped cream*, ground cinnamon
Vanilla beans (optional)

Combine first 6 ingredients in a Dutch oven. Cook over medium heat 10 minutes or until chocolate melts and sugar dissolves, stirring occasionally. Remove from heat, and whisk vigorously until hot chocolate is frothy.

Immediately pour into mugs; stir a splash of coffee liqueur into each serving, if desired. Top with whipped cream, and sprinkle with cinnamon, if desired. Add a vanilla bean to each mug as a stirrer stick, if desired. **Yield: 11 cups.**

*We tested with canned Reddi-wip topping. For party fun, it's quick and easy, and fun to squirt.

Healthy
Holiday Menus

These recipes show that you can hold the fat and calories at bay and still enjoy a grand holiday meal. Each recipe includes a nutrient analysis—as well as a great flavor profile.

Elegant Dinner for Eight

Peppered Beef Tenderloin Medallions with
Olive-Herb Relish

Sun-dried Tomato and Garlic Whipped Potatoes

Green Beans with Roasted Mushrooms

Cran-Ginger Granita

game plan

1 week ahead:
• Prepare and freeze Cran-Ginger Granita.

1 day ahead:
• Steam green beans; cover and chill.
• Prepare Sun-dried Tomato and Garlic Whipped Potatoes; cover and chill.
• Make Olive-Herb Relish; cover and chill.

2 hours ahead:
• Roast mushrooms.

15 minutes ahead:
• Roast beef medallions.

Last Minute:
• Reheat whipped potatoes in microwave.
• Toss together green beans and mushrooms, and reheat in microwave.

After Dinner:
• Scrape frozen granita until fluffy. Spoon into serving dishes.

editor's favorite • low calorie • low carb

Peppered Beef Tenderloin Medallions with Olive-Herb Relish

A pair of these mouthwatering tender little medallions topped with tangy olives makes a luxurious entrée.

Prep: 6 min.   Cook: 14 min.

16   (3-oz.) beef tenderloin fillets*
2   tsp. crushed black peppercorns
2   tsp. crushed pink peppercorns
1   tsp. kosher salt
¼   cup olive oil
Olive-Herb Relish

Sprinkle fillets with peppercorns and salt.

Heat 2 Tbsp. oil in each of 2 large skillets (preferably cast iron) over medium-high heat. Sear fillets in hot oil over medium-high heat 2 minutes on each side. Arrange beef medallions in a single layer on a large baking sheet lined with aluminum foil.

Bake at 400° for 6 to 10 minutes or until desired degree of doneness. Serve with Olive-Herb Relish. **Yield: 8 servings.**

Per serving and 2 Tbsp. relish: Calories 315 (62% from fat); Fat 21.6g (sat 5.6g, mono 12g, poly 1.6g); Protein 27.2g; Carb 1.8g; Fiber 0.6g; Chol 80mg; Iron 3.9mg; Sodium 543mg; Calc 18mg

*Ask your butcher to cut 3-oz. petit beef fillets (medallions) from the slender end of several tenderloins. This will ensure that you end up with 16 medallions not over 3 oz. each.

Olive-Herb Relish

Prep: 8 min.   Other: 2 hr.

½   cup pitted kalamata olives, chopped
½   cup pitted Manzanilla green olives, chopped
½   cup roasted red bell peppers, diced
2   Tbsp. chopped fresh tarragon
2   Tbsp. capers, drained
1   Tbsp. extra-virgin olive oil

Combine all ingredients in a small bowl; stir well. Cover and chill at least 2 hours. **Yield: 1½ cups.**

Per Tbsp.: Calories 19 (85% from fat); Fat 1.8g (sat 0.2g, mono 1.4g, poly 0.2g); Protein 0.1g; Carb 0.6g; Fiber 0.1g; Chol 0mg; Iron 0.1mg; Sodium 124mg; Calc 4mg

Sun-dried Tomato and Garlic Whipped Potatoes

Tangy tomato bits and a subtle garlic flavor enhance these fluffy spuds.

Prep: 12 min.   Cook: 20 min.

3	lb. Yukon gold potatoes, peeled and cut into chunks
¼	cup dried tomatoes packed in oil, drained
4	large garlic cloves
1½	cups 2% reduced-fat milk
2	Tbsp. light butter
1	tsp. salt
1	tsp. pepper

Cook potatoes in boiling water to cover 15 to 20 minutes or until tender; drain well.

Meanwhile, place dried tomatoes and garlic cloves in a mini food processor; process until finely minced. Combine milk and butter in a glass bowl. Partially cover with heavy-duty plastic wrap, and microwave at HIGH 1½ to 2 minutes or until butter is melted. Combine potatoes, warm milk, and salt and pepper in a large bowl. Beat at medium speed with an electric mixer until potatoes are fluffy. Gently stir in dried tomatoes and garlic. **Yield: 8 servings.**

Per serving: Calories 183 (15% from fat); Fat 3g (sat 1.5g, mono 0.6g, poly 0.2g); Protein 4.6g; Carb 35.9g; Fiber 3.2g; Chol 7mg; Iron 0.7mg; Sodium 355mg; Calc 74mg

Make Ahead: Cover and chill prepared potatoes overnight. Microwave at HIGH 5 to 7 minutes to reheat.

Green Beans with Roasted Mushrooms

The roasted mushrooms tossed with slender French green beans make a rich but light side dish. Regular green beans and button mushrooms can be substituted.

Prep: 7 min.   Cook: 30 min.

2	lb. haricots verts, trimmed
1½	lb. assorted mushrooms, quartered (we tested with 6 [4-oz.] packages of Gourmet Mushroom Blend)
2	Tbsp. balsamic vinegar, divided
2	Tbsp. extra-virgin olive oil
1	Tbsp. chopped fresh thyme
½	tsp. salt
½	tsp. freshly ground black pepper

Place green beans in a large pot of boiling water, and cook 3 to 4 minutes or until crisp-tender. Immediately plunge into ice water to stop the cooking process. Cover and chill up to 2 days.

Combine mushrooms, 1 Tbsp. vinegar, and next 4 ingredients on a large rimmed baking sheet coated with cooking spray. Spread mushrooms in a single layer.

Roast at 425° for 20 to 25 minutes or until tender and browned, stirring once or twice. Reheat green beans in the microwave at HIGH 3 minutes or until hot. Combine green beans, roasted mushrooms, and remaining 1 Tbsp. vinegar; toss well. **Yield: 8 servings.**

Per serving: Calories 84 (42% from fat); Fat 3.9g (sat 0.6g, mono 2.7g, poly 0.5g); Protein 4.5g; Carb 10.6g; Fiber 4.3g; Chol 0mg; Iron 1.6mg; Sodium 157mg; Calc 42mg

Cran-Ginger Granita

(pictured on page 136)

Prep: 6 min.   Other: 4 hr.

3	cups cranberry-apple juice drink, divided
½	cup sugar
1	(12-oz.) can natural ginger ale (we tested with Natural Brew Outrageous Ginger Ale)*

Combine 1 cup cranberry-apple juice drink and sugar in a 2-qt. saucepan. Cook over medium heat until sugar dissolves. Remove from heat and cool completely.

Combine cran-syrup, remaining 2 cups juice drink, and ginger ale. Pour into 3 ice cube trays, and freeze 1½ hours or until almost frozen. Transfer cubes to a blender or food processor, and pulse until slushy.

Pour slush into a 13" x 9" pan, and freeze 3½ hours or until frozen.

To serve, scrape granita in pan with tines of a fork until fluffy. Spoon into dessert glasses, and serve immediately. **Yield: 8 cups.**

Per 1-cup serving: Calories 124 (0% from fat); Fat 0g (sat 0g, mono 0g, poly 0g); Protein 0.1g; Carb 31.9g; Fiber 0.1g; Chol 0mg; Iron 0.1mg; Sodium 5mg; Calc 8mg

*Natural ginger ale has an intense gingery taste. Find it on the soft drink aisle or with beers, especially in upscale markets.

Winter Harvest

Broccoli Pesto

Fennel and Parmesan Salad

Rosemary-Dijon Roast Pork with
Autumn Fruit Compote

Parsnip and Potato Mash

Lemon-Drenched Gingerbread Cake

menu for 8

game plan

2 days ahead:
• Prepare Autumn Fruit Compote; cover and chill.

1 day ahead:
• Make Broccoli Pesto; cover and chill. Toast bread, and store in an airtight container.
• Wash Bibb lettuce, grate cheese, and make dressing for Fennel and Parmesan Salad; chill separately.
• Bake Lemon-Drenched Gingerbread Cake; store at room temperature in an airtight container.

1 hour ahead:
• Bake pork roast.
• Make Parsnip and Potato Mash; keep warm.

Last minute:
• Assemble pesto and bread for serving.
• Toss Fennel and Parmesan Salad.
• Garnish cake for serving.

editor's favorite • low calorie • low carb • quick & easy

Broccoli Pesto

Traditional pesto is made with fresh basil. Broccoli replaces basil in this version, giving the pesto the same beautiful green color and an even healthier result. We served it on baguette slices; it's also great tossed with hot cooked pasta. It also makes a nice base for pizza.

Prep: 14 min.   Cook: 10 min.

1   (12-oz.) bag fresh broccoli florets, rinsed and drained
⅓   cup extra-virgin olive oil
4   garlic cloves, thinly sliced
⅛   tsp. dried crushed red pepper
⅓   cup freshly grated Parmesan cheese
¼   cup pine nuts, toasted
⅓   cup chicken broth
2   Tbsp. fresh lemon juice
½   tsp. salt
Garnish: toasted pine nuts
Toasted or grilled baguette slices

   Place broccoli in a large bowl; cover with heavy-duty plastic wrap. Microwave at HIGH 8 minutes or until broccoli is tender. Drain and transfer broccoli to a food processor.
   While broccoli cooks, heat olive oil in a small skillet over medium heat. Add garlic and crushed red pepper; sauté 2 minutes until garlic is lightly browned. Add garlic mixture, Parmesan cheese, and next 4 ingredients to food processor; process until smooth. Cover and refrigerate up to 2 days. Garnish, if desired. Serve pesto with baguette slices. **Yield: 2 cups.**

Per 1 Tbsp. pesto and 1 (¼"-thick) baguette slice: Calories 49 (62% from fat); Fat 3.4g (sat 0.5g, mono 1.9g, poly 0.7g); Protein 1.3g; Carb 4.1g; Fiber 0.5g; Chol 1mg; Iron 0.3mg; Sodium 103mg; Calc 15mg

Fennel and Parmesan Salad

Fresh lemon flavor carries this recipe. Buy the whole fennel, and use the feathery fronds, which look like dill, to add that herby punch to the salad.

Prep: 25 min.

2   fennel bulbs with stalks (about 2½ lb.)
2   tsp. grated lemon rind
2   Tbsp. fresh lemon juice (about 1 large)
2   Tbsp. extra-virgin olive oil
½   tsp. salt
¼   tsp. freshly ground pepper
1   large head Bibb lettuce, torn (6 cups)
¾   cup freshly shredded Parmesan cheese

Trim stalks from fennel, reserving feathery fronds. Quarter fennel bulbs vertically, discarding cores. Cut each quarter into ⅛" lengthwise slices. Chop fronds to measure ¼ cup, discarding remaining fronds.

Whisk together lemon rind and next 4 ingredients in a large bowl. Add fennel, fennel fronds, lettuce, and cheese; toss well. Divide salad among 8 serving plates. Serve immediately. **Yield: 8 servings.**

Per serving: Calories 100 (53% from fat); Fat 5.9g (sat 1.8g, mono 3.2g, poly 0.6g); Protein 4.7g; Carb 9.1g; Fiber 3.7g; Chol 5mg; Iron 1.3mg; Sodium 328mg; Calc 160mg

Rosemary-Dijon Roast Pork with Autumn Fruit Compote

Searing this roast in a hot skillet kick-starts that sought-after crusty, caramelized exterior.

Prep: 5 min. Cook: 55 min. Other: 10 min.

1   (2½-lb.) boneless pork loin roast, trimmed
¾   tsp. salt
½   tsp. freshly ground pepper
1   Tbsp. olive oil
3   Tbsp. Dijon mustard
2   Tbsp. chopped fresh rosemary
Autumn Fruit Compote

Pat pork roast dry with paper towels. Sprinkle or rub roast with salt and pepper.

Heat oil in a large heavy skillet over medium-high heat. Brown pork roast on all sides, about 5 minutes total. Place roast on a rack in a lightly greased roasting pan.

Combine mustard and 2 Tbsp. rosemary; spread onto browned pork.

Bake, uncovered, at 350° for 45 to 55 minutes or until a thermometer inserted in center of roast registers 155°. Cover with aluminum foil, and let stand 10 minutes or until thermometer registers 160° before slicing. Serve with Autumn Fruit Compote. **Yield: 8 servings.**

Per serving with ⅓ cup compote: Calories 290 (25% from fat); Fat 8.1g (sat 2.5g, mono 3.8g, poly 0.8g); Protein 29.3g; Carb 25g; Fiber 2.2g; Chol 81mg; Iron 2.1mg; Sodium 351mg; Calc 26mg

Autumn Fruit Compote

Prep: 12 min. Cook: 16 min. Other: 2 hr.

4   (3") fresh rosemary sprigs
½   tsp. black peppercorns, crushed
1   cup orange juice
¼   cup firmly packed brown sugar
2   Bartlett pears, peeled and sliced
2   Granny Smith apples, peeled and sliced
½   cup dried apricots
½   cup golden raisins
½   cup fresh cranberries

Place rosemary and crushed peppercorns in a small square of cheesecloth; tie to secure. Place cheesecloth bag, orange juice, and next 6 ingredients in a large saucepan; bring to a boil over medium-high heat. Reduce heat to medium-low; cover and simmer 8 minutes or until apple and pear are almost tender. Remove from heat, and let cool to room temperature. Remove and discard cheesecloth. **Yield: 3¾ cups.**

Per tablespoon: Calories 18 (0% from fat); Fat 0g (sat 0g, mono 0g, poly 0g); Protein 0.2g; Carb 4.6g; Fiber 0.4g; Chol 0mg; Iron 0.1mg; Sodium 1mg; Calc 3mg

Make-Ahead Note: Compote can be prepared at least 2 days in advance and stored in refrigerator. Bring to room temperature before serving.

Parsnip and Potato Mash

No more cold mashed potatoes—pour hot water in a serving bowl, and let sit for a minute or two before dinner. Drain the bowl, wipe it dry, and then add hot potatoes.

Prep: 16 min. Cook: 32 min.

2   lb. parsnips, peeled and cut into 1" pieces
2   lb. baking potatoes, peeled and cut into
    1" pieces
2   Tbsp. butter
½   cup 2% reduced-fat milk
1   tsp. salt
¼   tsp. freshly ground pepper

Place parsnips and potatoes in a Dutch oven; cover with 1" water. Bring to a boil; cover, reduce heat, and simmer 25 minutes or until vegetables are tender. Drain vegetables, and return to hot pan.

Add butter, and mash vegetables using a potato masher. Add milk, salt, and pepper. Mash. Serve warm. **Yield: about 7 cups.**

Per ¾-cup serving: Calories 175 (16% from fat); Fat 3.1g (sat 1.8g, mono 0.8g, poly 0.2g); Protein 3.1g; Carb 35.1g; Fiber 5.9g; Chol 8mg; Iron 0.8mg; Sodium 296mg; Calc 56mg

Lemon-Drenched Gingerbread Cake

Prep: 12 min. Cook: 35 min. Other: 15 min.

¾   cup molasses
⅔   cup firmly packed light brown sugar
½   cup canola oil
1   large egg
2½   cups all-purpose flour
1   Tbsp. ground ginger
2   tsp. baking powder
1   tsp. baking soda
1   tsp. ground cinnamon
1   tsp. ground cloves
½   tsp. salt
1   cup hot water
½   cup granulated sugar
⅔   cup water
2   Tbsp. fresh lemon juice
½   tsp. lemon extract
Powdered sugar
Garnish: lemon and orange rind

Coat a 10-cup Bundt pan with cooking spray.

Beat first 4 ingredients at medium speed with an electric mixer until blended.

Combine flour and next 6 ingredients; add to molasses mixture alternately with hot water, beginning and ending with flour mixture. Beat at low speed after each addition. Pour batter into prepared pan.

Bake at 350° for 32 to 35 minutes or until a long wooden pick inserted in center comes out clean. Cool cake in pan on a wire rack 15 minutes.

Meanwhile, combine ½ cup sugar, ⅔ cup water, lemon juice, and lemon extract in a small saucepan; simmer over medium-low heat 5 minutes, stirring to dissolve sugar. Remove from heat, and let cool 10 minutes.

Poke holes in top of cake using a skewer. Pour syrup over cake. Cool completely. Invert cake onto a serving platter; lightly sprinkle with powdered sugar. Garnish, if desired. **Yield: 12 servings.**

Per serving: Calories 328 (28% from fat); Fat 10.1g (sat 0.9g, mono 5.7g, poly 3g); Protein 3.3g; Carb 57.2g; Fiber 0.9g; Chol 18mg; Iron 2.7mg; Sodium 302mg; Calc 108mg

This is not an indulgent cake—no butter and only one egg; however, you'll think it is because it soaks in a lemon syrup and becomes gooey good.

Lemon-Drenched Gingerbread Cake

Holiday's Finest

Dried Fig and Blue Cheese Salad with
Pomegranate Vinaigrette

Crab Cakes with Lemon-Parsley Slaw

Ambrosia with Meringues

menu for 6

game plan

1 day ahead:
• Prepare dried figs and pomegranate vinaigrette, and wash greens for Dried Fig and Blue Cheese Salad with Pomegranate Vinaigrette; chill.
• Make dressing for Lemon-Parsley Slaw; chill.
• Prepare fruit for ambrosia; chill.

4 hours ahead:
• Shape crab cakes, place on a baking sheet; cover and chill.

Last minute:
• Slice fennel, and assemble Dried Fig and Blue Cheese Salad with Pomegranate Vinaigrette.
• Bake crab cakes.
• Toss together ingredients for Lemon-Parsley Slaw.

Crab Cakes with
Lemon-Parsley
Slaw

Ambrosia with Meringues

editor's favorite • make ahead • quick & easy

Dried Fig and Blue Cheese Salad with Pomegranate Vinaigrette

Not only is the vinaigrette good for you with antioxidants in the pomegranate juice, it's an impressive salad to serve guests.

Prep: 6 min.   Cook: 19 min.

18   dried mission figs
1   (16-oz.) bottle pomegranate juice (2 cups)
2   Tbsp. honey
1   tsp. Dijon mustard
¼   tsp. salt
¼   tsp. freshly ground pepper
¼   cup olive oil
9   cups mesclun salad greens
2   oz. blue cheese, crumbled

   Place figs and pomegranate juice in a medium saucepan; bring to a boil. Reduce heat, cover, and simmer 10 minutes or until figs are softened. Remove figs with a slotted spoon; set aside.

Bring pomegranate juice to a boil over medium-high heat; boil 2 minutes or until syrupy and reduced to ⅓ cup. Transfer reduction to a bowl; let cool to room temperature.

Add honey and next 3 ingredients to pomegranate reduction; stir with a wire whisk. Gradually whisk in oil.

To serve, divide mesclun greens among 6 serving plates; top each salad with 3 figs. Drizzle evenly with vinaigrette, and sprinkle with blue cheese. Serve immediately. **Yield: 6 servings.**

Per serving: Calories 345 (33% from fat); Fat 12.8g (sat 3.4g, mono 7.5g, poly 1.2g); Protein 5.7g; Carb 58.2g; Fiber 7.6g; Chol 8mg; Iron 2.1mg; Sodium 311mg; Calc 166mg

Make-Ahead Note: Cooked figs and vinaigrette can be stored in refrigerator up to 2 days.

low calorie • low carb • low fat

Crab Cakes with Lemon-Parsley Slaw

Get the crispy brown crust on these crab cakes with our easy oven procedure.

Prep: 15 min.   Cook: 20 min.

1½   lb. fresh crabmeat
½   cup panko or other breadcrumbs, divided
2   Tbsp. reduced-fat mayonnaise
1   large egg
1   Tbsp. minced chives
1   Tbsp. Dijon mustard
1   tsp. Old Bay seasoning
Vegetable cooking spray
Lemon wedges
Lemon-Parsley Slaw

Preheat oven to 450°.

Place a jelly-roll pan in oven 10 minutes to heat.

Drain and flake crabmeat, removing any bits of shell.

Combine ¼ cup breadcrumbs, mayonnaise, and next 4 ingredients; gently add crabmeat to mixture using hands to toss. Shape into 12 small patties. Dredge patties in remaining ¼ cup breadcrumbs.

Coat crab cakes well with cooking spray. Remove hot pan from oven; coat pan with cooking spray. Place crab cakes on hot pan in a single layer. Bake at 450° for 10 minutes; turn cakes over and bake 10 more minutes or until lightly browned. Serve with lemon wedges and Lemon-Parsley Slaw. **Yield: 6 servings.**

Per 2 crab cakes and ¾ cup slaw: Calories 187 (40% from fat); Fat 8.4g (sat 1.1g, mono 3.9g, poly 0.6g); Protein 18.9g; Carb 9.2g; Fiber 1.9g; Chol 137mg; Iron 1.5mg; Sodium 1037mg; Calc 61mg

Lemon-Parsley Slaw

Prep: 4 min.

2   tsp. grated lemon rind
1   tsp. fresh lemon juice
½   tsp. Dijon mustard
½   tsp. salt
2   Tbsp. extra-virgin olive oil
6   cups angel hair slaw or thinly sliced cabbage
1   cup chopped fresh flat-leaf parsley

Whisk together first 4 ingredients in a large bowl: gradually whisk in olive oil. Add slaw and parsley, tossing gently to coat. Serve immediately. **Yield: 6 servings.**

Per ¾ cup slaw: Calories 63 (69% from fat); Fat 4.8g (sat 0.7g, mono 3.6g, poly 0.4g); Protein 1g; Carb 4.2g; Fiber 1.7g; Chol 0mg; Iron 0.6mg; Sodium 218mg; Calc 15mg

low calorie • low cholesterol • low fat • quick & easy

Ambrosia with Meringues

Store-bought meringue kiss cookies provide a simple garnish and sweet crunch for holiday fruit.

Prep: 22 min.

1   cup fresh cranberries
½   cup sugar
½   cup water
4   large navel oranges
2   cups fresh pineapple chunks (½" chunks)
⅓   cup sweetened flaked coconut
12   prebaked meringue cookies

Combine first 3 ingredients in a medium saucepan; cook, stirring often, over medium heat 6 to 8 minutes or until most of cranberries pop. Grate 1 Tbsp. plus 1 tsp. orange rind from oranges.

Remove cranberries from heat, and stir in 1 tsp. orange rind. Let cranberries cool completely. Cover and refrigerate.

Section oranges over a large bowl, catching juices. Add pineapple and 1 Tbsp. orange rind to orange sections in bowl. Cover and chill until ready to serve.

To serve, spoon oranges and pineapple into individual dessert dishes; top evenly with cranberry mixture. Sprinkle each serving with coconut. Serve with meringue cookies. **Yield: 6 servings.**

Per serving: Calories 216 (6% from fat); Fat 1.5g (sat 1.2g, mono 0.1g, poly 0.1g); Protein 1.5g; Carb 51.3g; Fiber 4.6g; Chol 0mg; Iron 0.5mg; Sodium 21mg; Calc 53mg

Crispy Chocolate Popcorn,
Holiday Fortune Cookies

Snacks & Munchies *Swap*

Move over cookie swap; this get-together encourages savory or sweet pick-up food of all kinds to sample and share with friends.

Rocky Road Granola Clusters

Look for sesame sticks in grocery markets that sell bulk nuts, candies, and snack mixes.

Prep: 20 min.   Cook: 5 min.

1   (16-oz.) package chocolate candy coating, chopped
2   Tbsp. shortening
¼   cup creamy peanut butter
2   to 3 cups coarsely chopped granola bars (we tested with Nature Valley Maple Brown Sugar Granola Bars)
¾   cup sesame sticks or thin pretzels
3   Tbsp. slivered almonds, toasted
1   cup miniature marshmallows
12 caramels, chopped

Combine chocolate coating and shortening in a large microwave-safe bowl; cover loosely with heavy-duty plastic wrap. Microwave at HIGH 1½ minutes or until melted, stirring once. Stir in peanut butter. Let stand 2 minutes. Stir in granola bars, sesame sticks, and almonds. Stir in marshmallows and caramels last so they don't melt. Drop by rounded tablespoonfuls onto parchment or wax paper. Let clusters stand until firm. **Yield: 2 dozen.**

Package these clusters or chocolate popcorn in decorative boxes. Line them with wax paper or tissue, or wrap boxes in cellophane.

Rocky Road Granola Clusters

Crispy Chocolate Popcorn

editor's favorite • gift idea

Crispy Chocolate Popcorn

Prep: 30 min.   Cook: 1 hr.

2	cups milk chocolate morsels, divided
1½	cups firmly packed light brown sugar
¾	cup butter
¾	cup light corn syrup
¾	tsp. salt
1½	tsp. vanilla extract
¾	tsp. baking soda
2	(3.5-oz.) bags natural-flavored microwave popcorn, popped
2	cups peanuts or cashews

Combine 1 cup chocolate morsels, brown sugar, and next 3 ingredients in a heavy saucepan; cook over medium heat, stirring constantly, until mixture come to a boil. Remove from heat, and stir in vanilla and baking soda.

Distribute popcorn and nuts evenly into 2 lightly greased roasting pans. Be sure to remove all unpopped kernels of popcorn before pouring chocolate mixture over popcorn. Pour chocolate mixture evenly over popcorn and nuts, stirring well with a lightly greased spatula.

Bake at 250° for 1 hour, stirring every 15 minutes. Spread on wax paper to cool, breaking apart large clumps as mixture cools. Sprinkle remaining 1 cup chocolate morsels evenly over hot popcorn; let cool. Store in airtight containers. **Yield: about 29 cups.**

Christmas Gorp

Prep: 25 min.

1½ cups white chocolate baking morsels
¾ cup creamy peanut butter
¼ cup plus 2 Tbsp. butter
1 Tbsp. honey
¼ tsp. ground cinnamon (optional)
8 cups crispy corn and rice cereal squares (we tested with Crispix)
1 (8-oz.) package pretzel-flavored fish-shaped crackers (3 cups)
1½ cups powdered sugar
2 cups salted, roasted almonds with skins
2 cups red and green candy-coated chocolate pieces
1½ cups sweetened dried cranberries or raisins

Combine first 4 ingredients and cinnamon, if desired, in a heavy saucepan. Cook over medium heat, stirring until morsels and butter melt. Place cereal and crackers in a large bowl; add melted white chocolate mixture. Stir until well coated. Let cool slightly.

Place powdered sugar in a large zip-top plastic bag. Add coated cereal mixture in batches; seal bag, and toss well to coat. Combine sugar-coated cereal mixture, almonds, and remaining ingredients in a large bowl. Stir gently to blend. Store in an airtight container. **Yield: 18 cups.**

Package these festive fortune cookies (shown at right) in those familiar to-go cartons. The cartons are available in a variety of colors online or at your local party store.

Holiday Fortune Cookies

Wear gloves while shaping these fortune cookies fresh from the oven. They cool and crisp quickly, so bake and shape them two at a time. Bake more at one time if you have helpers. To make paper fortunes, type them, triple spaced, on a computer. Cut them out, fold in half, and place in middle of cookies before folding.

Prep: 5 min.   Cook: 12 min. per batch

½ cup all-purpose flour
1 Tbsp. cornstarch
¼ cup sugar
¼ tsp. salt
¼ tsp. ground cinnamon
⅛ tsp. ground nutmeg
¼ cup canola oil
2 large egg whites
1 Tbsp. water
1 tsp. vanilla extract
2 (2-oz.) vanilla candy coating squares
Red decorator sugar
Purple decorator sugar

Whisk together first 6 ingredients in a medium bowl. Add oil and egg whites, whisking until smooth. Whisk in water and vanilla extract.

Drop a rounded teaspoonful of batter onto a well-greased baking sheet. Using back of a spoon, spread batter into a 3" circle. Repeat procedure with another rounded teaspoonful of batter. Bake at 300° for 10 to 12 minutes or until light golden brown.

Working quickly, immediately remove each cookie from pan with a spatula, and flip over into gloved hand; place prepared fortune in center of each cookie and fold each cookie in half. Grasp end of each cookie, and place over the edge of a bowl, drawing the edges down to form a crease. Place cookies, ends down, in muffin pans to maintain shape; let cookies cool completely. Repeat procedure with remaining batter, baking 2 cookies at a time.

To decorate, microwave vanilla coating in a small bowl at MEDIUM (50% power) 2 minutes, stirring after 1 minute. Dip outer edge of each cookie in vanilla coating, and then into red or purple sugar; set aside to let coating harden. **Yield: about 2 dozen.**

Holiday Fortune
Cookies

▲ Place paper fortune in center of cookie, and quickly fold cookie in half.

▲ Grasp end of each cookie, and place over the edge of a bowl, drawing the edges down to form a crease.

▲ Place cookies, ends down, in muffin pans to set the shape.

Who doesn't love a thin, crisp pita chip? Take your pick from this fun mix of flavor possibilities.

Bacon, Cheddar, and Ranch Pita Chips; Parmesan-Herb Pita Chips

make ahead • quick & easy

Barbecue Pita Chips

Prep: 6 min. Cook: 15 min.

¼   cup butter, melted
1½   Tbsp. barbecue seasoning (we tested with McCormick's Grill Mates)
1½   Tbsp. lemon juice
3   (6") pita rounds

Combine butter, barbecue seasoning, and lemon juice in a small bowl.

Split each pita bread into 2 rounds. Cut each round into 8 wedges. Place wedges on a lightly greased baking sheet. Brush rough side of each wedge with butter mixture. Bake at 350° for 15 minutes or until crisp. Remove from oven; transfer to wire racks to cool. **Yield: 4 dozen chips.**

make ahead • quick & easy

Bacon, Cheddar, and Ranch Pita Chips

Prep: 6 min. Cook: 15 min.

¼   cup olive oil
1½   Tbsp. Ranch dressing mix
3   (6") pita rounds
⅓   cup real bacon bits (we tested with Hormel)
½   cup (2 oz.) shredded sharp Cheddar cheese

Combine olive oil and dressing mix in a small bowl.

Split each pita bread into 2 rounds. Cut each round into 8 wedges. Place wedges on a lightly greased baking sheet. Brush rough side of each wedge with oil mixture. Sprinkle wedges with bacon bits and then cheese. Bake at 350° for 15 minutes or until crisp. Remove from oven; transfer to wire racks to cool. **Yield: 4 dozen chips.**

Taco Pita Chips

Prep: 6 min.   Cook: 15 min.

¼   cup olive oil
1½   Tbsp. taco seasoning
3   (6") pita rounds
1   (8-oz.) package shredded Mexican four-cheese blend

Combine olive oil and taco seasoning in a small bowl.
Split each pita bread into 2 rounds. Cut each round into 8 wedges. Place wedges on a lightly greased baking sheet. Brush rough side of each wedge with oil mixture. Sprinkle wedges with cheese. Bake at 350° for 15 minutes or until crisp. Remove from oven; transfer to wire racks to cool. **Yield: 4 dozen chips.**

make ahead • quick & easy

Parmesan-Herb Pita Chips

Prep: 6 min.   Cook: 15 min.

⅓   cup olive oil
4   tsp. dried Italian seasoning
1   tsp. garlic salt
3   (6") pita rounds
½   cup freshly grated Parmesan cheese

Combine olive oil, Italian seasoning, and garlic salt.
Split each pita bread into 2 rounds. Cut each round into 8 wedges. Place wedges on a lightly greased baking sheet. Brush rough side of each wedge with oil mixture. Sprinkle wedges with cheese. Bake at 350° for 15 minutes or until crisp. Transfer to wire racks to cool. **Yield: 4 dozen chips.**

make ahead • quick & easy

Sea Salt and Cracked Pepper Pita Chips

Prep: 6 min.   Cook: 15 min.

3   (6") pita rounds
¼   cup olive oil
½   tsp. sea salt
½   tsp. freshly ground black pepper

Split each pita bread into 2 rounds. Cut each round into 8 wedges. Place wedges on a lightly greased baking sheet. Brush rough side of each wedge with oil. Sprinkle with salt and pepper. Bake at 350° for 15 minutes or until crisp. Transfer to wire racks to cool. **Yield: 4 dozen chips.**

make ahead

Famous Sausage Ball Muffins

This recipe has been around for years, and every cook has definite opinions and memories related to it. We found the recipe fun to revisit as easy mini muffins and with some flavor variations.

Prep: 5 min.   Cook: 15 min. per batch

2   cups all-purpose baking mix
1   lb. hot or regular pork sausage (we tested with Jimmy Dean)
2   cups (8 oz.) shredded sharp Cheddar cheese (we tested with Cracker Barrel)

Combine all ingredients in a large bowl, pressing together with hands. Spoon rounded tablespoonfuls into lightly greased 1¾" miniature muffin pans. Bake at 400° for 13 to 15 minutes or until lightly browned. Remove from pans, and serve warm with desired sauce, such as Ranch dressing, honey mustard, or barbecue sauce. **Yield: 4 dozen.**

Note: To make traditional Sausage Balls, shape mixture into ¾" balls, and place on ungreased baking sheets. Bake at 400° for 15 to 18 minutes or until lightly browned. **Yield: about 8 dozen.** Freeze uncooked sausage balls, if desired. Bake frozen balls for 18 to 20 minutes.

Dressed-Up Sausage Ball Muffins: Add ⅓ cup finely chopped onion, 1 Tbsp. garlic powder, and ¼ tsp. hot sauce to sausage-cheese dough. Proceed with recipe. **Yield: 4 dozen.**

Southwest Sausage Ball Muffins: Use Pepper Jack cheese instead of Cheddar, and add 1 (4.5-oz.) can chopped green chiles, drained and patted dry with paper towels, to sausage-cheese dough. Bake 20 minutes. **Yield: about 4½ dozen.**

Mediterranean Sausage Ball Muffins: Add ⅔ cup chopped pimiento-stuffed green olives. Use 1 cup Cheddar cheese and 1 cup crumbled feta cheese. Proceed with recipe. **Yield: about 4½ dozen.**

Sausage Ball Cocktail: Skewer 2 or 3 warm Sausage Balls onto a small wooden pick or skewer. Spoon a few Tbsp. Ranch dressing into a martini glass; add skewered sausage balls.

Giving

Make, bake, wrap, and present your best gifts
this holiday season.

Gifts *from* the Kitchen

Homemade goodies like these taste best when delivered with love during the holiday season.

Smoked Sea Salt Chocolate-Covered Turtles

Savor the best of both salty and sweet in each bite of these unique candies.

Prep: 25 min.   Cook: 25 min.   Other: 45 min.

1   (14-oz.) package caramels
2   Tbsp. butter
2   Tbsp. water
3   cups pecan halves, toasted
8   (2-oz.) chocolate candy coating squares
1   cup bittersweet chocolate morsels
4   (1-oz.) bittersweet chocolate baking squares
2   Tbsp. shortening
Smoked sea salt (see note)

Combine first 3 ingredients in a heavy saucepan over low heat, stirring constantly, until smooth. Stir in pecan halves. Remove from heat; cool in pan 5 minutes.

Drop candy by tablespoonfuls onto a jelly-roll pan lined with lightly greased wax paper. Freeze 30 minutes.

Melt chocolates and shortening in a heavy saucepan over low heat, stirring until smooth. Dip caramel candies into chocolate mixture, 4 or 5 at a time, allowing excess chocolate to drip off; place on lightly greased wax paper. Quickly sprinkle tops with sea salt. Chill until firm. **Yield: 2 dozen.**

Note: McCormick smoked flavor sea salt grinder is readily available and is what we first tested and tasted on this candy. Then we went online and found some other fine options. See Halen Môn salt below and how to order on page 171.

Double Chocolate-Covered Toffee Grahams

Recapture delicious memories with this nostalgic snack— crisp graham crackers dunked in chocolate.

Prep: 20 min.   Cook: 4 min.   Other: 20 min.

2   sleeves graham crackers (18 whole crackers)
6   (2-oz.) vanilla candy coating squares, cut in half
4   (1-oz.) white chocolate baking squares, chopped
4   Tbsp. shortening, divided
6   (2-oz.) chocolate candy coating squares, cut in half
4   (1-oz.) semisweet chocolate baking squares, chopped
½   cup toffee bits

Break each graham cracker in half.

Place vanilla squares, white chocolate squares, and 2 Tbsp. shortening in a microwave-safe bowl. Microwave at HIGH 1 to 2 minutes or until white chocolate is soft; stir until smooth. Dip 18 graham cracker squares entirely in melted white chocolate. Place dipped grahams on a parchment paper-lined baking sheet. Chill 20 minutes or until white chocolate is firm. Repeat procedure with chocolate squares, remaining 2 Tbsp. shortening, and remaining graham crackers. Drizzle any remaining semisweet chocolate and white chocolate over dipped grahams; sprinkle with toffee bits. Chill until firm. **Yield: 3 dozen.**

◀ Dip and sprinkle candies a few at a time so the salt will adhere before the chocolate hardens.

Pecan-Chocolate Chip Cookie Brittle

Prep: 17 min.   Cook: 19 min.

1½	cups all-purpose flour
1	tsp. baking powder
¼	tsp. baking soda
¼	tsp. salt
¾	cup butter, melted and cooled slightly
½	cup granulated sugar
⅓	cup firmly packed light brown sugar
1	tsp. vanilla extract
1	cup semisweet chocolate mini-morsels
1	cup pecan pieces, toasted (see note)
½	cup sweetened flaked coconut, toasted (see note)

Combine first 4 ingredients; set aside.

Stir together butter and next 3 ingredients in a large bowl; add flour mixture, stirring until smooth. Stir in chocolate morsels, pecans, and coconut. (Dough will look crumbly.)

Press dough evenly into a lightly greased 15" x 10" jelly-roll pan, pressing almost to edges.

Bake at 350° for 19 minutes or until lightly browned and cookie "slab" seems crisp. Cool completely in pan. Break cookie into pieces. **Yield: 1 to 2 dozen cookie pieces.**

Note: You can toast pecan pieces and coconut in the same pan at 350° for 8 minutes.

Chipotle-Chocolate Toffee

This candy has an awesome flavor surprise—not for the fainthearted. (pictured on page 130)

Prep: 6 min.   Cook: 30 min.

1¼	cups unsalted butter
1	cup granulated sugar
½	cup firmly packed light brown sugar
⅓	cup water
1	Tbsp. light corn syrup
½	tsp. salt
1	Tbsp. chopped chipotle pepper plus 1 Tbsp. adobo sauce from can
2	cups natural almonds with skins, coarsely chopped
1	cup dark chocolate or semisweet chocolate morsels

Melt butter in a 3-qt. heavy saucepan over medium-low heat. Add granulated sugar and next 4 ingredients; cook

Pecan-Chocolate Chip Cookie Brittle

We like the thought of calling this "brittle" because it's a big slab of crisp chocolate chip cookie that you break into irregular pieces after it bakes.

until sugars dissolve, stirring constantly. Attach candy thermometer to pan. Increase heat to medium; add chopped chipotle pepper and sauce. Cook, stirring often, at a gentle boil 10 minutes. Add almonds, and continue boiling and stirring for 10 minutes or until thermometer registers 290°.

Remove from heat. Carefully pour candy onto a buttered jelly-roll pan; spread candy to ¼" thickness. Sprinkle with chocolate morsels. Let stand 2 minutes or until chocolate melts; spread chocolate using an offset spatula. Cool until chocolate hardens. Break toffee into pieces. **Yield: 1¼ lb.**

Chocolate-Cherry Sugar-Crusted Shortbread

Prep: 8 min.   Cook: 40 min.   Other: 30 min.

1	cup butter, softened
½	cup powdered sugar
2½	cups all-purpose flour
⅛	tsp. salt
¼	cup semisweet chocolate mini-morsels
¼	cup finely chopped dried cherries
1	tsp. vanilla extract
1	Tbsp. granulated sugar
½	cup granulated sugar

Beat butter at medium speed with an electric mixer until creamy; add powdered sugar, beating well.

Combine flour and salt; gradually add to butter mixture, beating until well blended. Stir in chocolate mini-morsels, cherries, and vanilla.

Line an 8" square pan with aluminum foil, allowing foil to extend over edges of pan. Lightly grease foil and sprinkle with 1 Tbsp. granulated sugar. Press dough into pan.

Bake at 325° for 40 minutes or until golden. Cool 30 minutes or until slightly warm in pan. Use foil to gently lift shortbread from pan. Cut shortbread into 1" squares using a sharp knife. Roll shortbread squares in ½ cup granulated sugar. **Yield: 64 cookies.**

Somewhat like little dessert croutons, these are great nibbles to enjoy with a cup of tea or cocoa.

Chocolate-Cherry Sugar-Crusted Shortbread

Kitchen Sink
Brownies

Coat a 13" x 9" pan with cooking spray. Line pan with aluminum foil, allowing ends to hang over short sides of pan. Tuck overlapping ends under rim on short sides. Coat foil with cooking spray; set pan aside.

Combine first 5 ingredients in a small bowl.

Beat butter and sugars at medium speed with an electric mixer until smooth; add eggs, coffee, and vanilla, beating just until blended. Add flour mixture; beat at medium speed until blended. Stir in sandwich cookie crumbs and remaining 4 ingredients.

Spoon batter into prepared pan, spreading evenly.

Bake at 325° for 55 to 58 minutes. Cool completely in pan on a wire rack. Cover and chill at least 2 hours.

Carefully invert brownies from pan using overlapping foil as handles; remove foil. Invert brownies again onto a cutting board. Cut brownies into squares. **Yield: 2 dozen.**

Note: We like this technique of lining a pan with foil before baking brownies. It sure makes cutting baked brownies neat and easy.

editor's favorite • gift idea • make ahead

Kitchen Sink Brownies

Decadence abounds in each bite of these chunky candy-studded brownies full of good things you've probably got in the pantry.

Prep: 22 min.   Cook: 58 min.   Other: 2 hr.

1½ cups all-purpose flour
1 cup unsweetened cocoa
½ tsp. baking powder
¼ tsp. baking soda
¼ tsp. salt
1½ cups butter, melted
1½ cups granulated sugar
1½ cups firmly packed light brown sugar
4 large eggs
¼ cup brewed espresso or French roast coffee
2 tsp. vanilla extract
1 cup chopped cream-filled chocolate sandwich cookies (10 cookies)
4 (1.45-oz.) milk chocolate candy bars with almonds, chopped (we tested with Hershey's)
½ cup dark chocolate morsels (we tested with Ghirardelli)
½ cup white chocolate morsels
1 cup pecan pieces, toasted

editor's favorite • gift idea

Cookie Biscotti Sticks

Liven up your next coffee break with these extravagant cookie sticks. They're impressive in size and mimic biscotti in length and crunch.

Prep: 11 min.   Cook: 26 min.   Other: 3 hr., 20 min.

1 cup firmly packed light brown sugar
⅔ cup butter
¼ cup light corn syrup
¼ cup creamy peanut butter
1 tsp. vanilla extract
3½ cups uncooked regular oats
1 (12-oz.) package semisweet chocolate morsels
1 cup butterscotch morsels
2 Tbsp. shortening
½ cup creamy peanut butter
½ cup coarsely chopped peanuts

Stir together brown sugar, butter, and corn syrup in a large saucepan; cook over medium heat until sugar dissolves and butter melts. Remove from heat. Stir in ¼ cup peanut butter and vanilla. Gently stir in oats. Press into bottom of an ungreased 13" x 9" pan lined with aluminum foil. Bake at 375° for 20 to 22 minutes or until browned.

Melt together chocolate morsels, butterscotch morsels, and shortening in a saucepan over medium heat, stirring until smooth; stir in ½ cup peanut butter. Spread over

Cookie Biscotti Sticks

baked cookie crust; sprinkle with peanuts. Let cool in pan on a wire rack 20 minutes. Cover and chill 2 to 3 hours or until firm. (Or pop them in the freezer to speed cooling. Just be sure to let them stand 5 minutes at room temperature before cutting.)

Lift uncut cookies out of pan using foil as handles. Cut crosswise into approximately 1"-thick sticks using a large chef's knife. Wrap in cellophane bags or plastic wrap for gift giving. **Yield: 1 dozen.**

◄ Use a sharp knife to cut through the crisp baked cookie crust. Work slowly so long cookie sticks don't crumble.

▲ Pair Pound Cake Minis and Fudgy Espresso Brownie Bites in holiday gift bags. Both are made using mini muffin pans.

Baby Pound Cakes

Enjoy these pound cake bites for breakfast or as a late-night snack by the fire, or split and toast them with butter. Vanilla bean paste, which can be found at specialty food stores, gives these cakes a sublime goodness. And just as with classic pound cake, we loved the crusty top edges on these, too.

Prep: 28 min.   Cook: 25 min.   Other: 10 min.

1½	cups butter, softened
1	(8-oz.) package cream cheese, softened
3	cups sugar
6	large eggs
3	cups all-purpose flour
¼	tsp. salt
1	Tbsp. vanilla bean paste or vanilla extract
½	tsp. almond extract

Beat butter and cream cheese at medium speed with an electric mixer about 2 minutes or until creamy. Gradually add sugar, beating well, 5 to 7 minutes. Add eggs, 1 at a time, beating just until yellow disappears.

Combine flour and salt. Gradually add to butter mixture, beating at low speed just until blended; stir in vanilla and almond flavorings. Spoon batter into paper-lined standard-size muffin pans, filling three-fourths full.

Bake at 350° for 22 to 25 minutes or until a wooden pick inserted in center comes out clean. Cool in pans on wire racks 10 minutes; remove from pans, and let cool completely on wire racks. **Yield: 2½ dozen.**

Pound Cake Minis:
Spoon batter into paper-lined (1¾") miniature muffin cups, filling three-fourths full. Bake at 350° for 16 to 18 minutes or until a wooden pick inserted in center comes out clean. Cool in pans on wire racks 10 minutes; remove from pans, and let cool completely on wire racks. **Yield: about 9 dozen.**

Fluted Baby Pound Cakes:
Spoon batter into a greased ¼-cup capacity mini fluted tube pan, filling three-fourths full. (We tested with a 12-cavity mini fluted tube pan.) Bake at 350° for 20 minutes or until a wooden pick inserted in center comes out clean. Cool in pans on wire racks 10 minutes; remove from pans, and let cool completely on wire racks. Dust with powdered sugar or drizzle with Jelly Bean Thumbprint Cookies glaze of powdered sugar and heavy cream (pg. 81), if desired. **Yield: 2½ dozen.**

Fudgy Espresso Brownie Bites

These petite brownies are rich and gooey, especially if you bake them the lesser time. You'd never guess they start with a mix. Pile some in a bag for gift giving.

Prep: 18 min.   Cook: 14 min.

1	Tbsp. espresso powder
¼	cup hot water
½	cup vegetable oil or canola oil
2	large eggs
1	(18.3-oz.) package fudge brownie mix (we tested with Betty Crocker)
1	cup semisweet chocolate morsels
1	cup coarsely chopped walnuts

Dissolve espresso powder in hot water in a 1-cup glass measuring cup, stirring with a small whisk. Cool slightly. Whisk in oil and eggs until blended.

Place brownie mix in a large bowl; break up large lumps with the back of a spoon. Stir in espresso mixture until blended. Stir in chocolate morsels and walnuts. Spoon mixture into 38 lightly greased (1¾") miniature muffin cups, filling full.

Bake at 375° for 12 to 14 minutes or until tops are shiny and crusty and centers are set. Cool completely in pans on wire racks. Remove from pans using a slight twisting motion. **Yield: 38 brownies.**

Fluted Baby Pound Cakes

Chai Tea Mix

For optimal enjoyment of this trendy flavor-packed drink, be sure your spices are fresh.

Prep: 14 min.

2½   tsp. ground ginger
2   tsp. ground cinnamon
¾   tsp. ground cloves
¾   tsp. ground cardamom (optional)
1   tsp. ground allspice
1   tsp. ground nutmeg
½   tsp. freshly ground black pepper
1½   cups unsweetened instant tea or decaffeinated instant tea
1½   to 2 cups sugar
1   cup nonfat dry milk powder
1   cup powdered nondairy creamer
1   cup French vanilla-flavored powdered nondairy creamer

Combine spices and tea in a food processor or blender. Blend 1 to 2 minutes or until mixture becomes a fine powder. Pour into a large bowl. Add sugar to food processor or blender (without cleaning it), and process until superfine, about 30 seconds. Add sugar to bowl of spices. Stir in milk powder and creamers; blend well. Spoon mix into gift jars, if desired.

To serve, stir 2 heaping Tbsp. Chai Tea Mix into a mug of hot milk or boiling water. **Yield: 5½ cups mix.**

Chocolate Chai Mix: Add ½ cup unsweetened cocoa along with dry milk powder to the blend above. Follow serving directions above. (We recommend milk here.)

Chai Shake: Blend ¼ cup Chai Tea Mix, 1 cup milk, and 3½ cups vanilla ice cream in a blender.

White Chocolate Chai: Add ¼ cup finely chopped premium white chocolate (such as Lindt or Ghirardelli) to 1 cup Chai Tea Mix. Stir well. Follow serving directions above with 2 heaping Tbsp. per cup of hot milk or boiling water.

Chai Shake

Chunky Tapenade

gift idea • make ahead • quick & easy

Chunky Tapenade

Serve this chunky French favorite as an hors d'oeuvre accompanied with baguette slices, enjoy it with pan-seared tuna or salmon, or on a sandwich of crusty bread and goat cheese. The recipe is easily doubled or tripled if you have multiple gifts to give.

Prep: 10 min.

½ cup pitted chopped kalamata olives
½ cup chopped pimiento-stuffed green olives
½ cup drained and chopped roasted red bell pepper
¼ cup olive oil
2 Tbsp. finely chopped fresh flat-leaf parsley
2 Tbsp. drained capers
1½ tsp. chopped fresh thyme
1¼ tsp. grated lemon rind
¼ tsp. freshly ground black pepper
2 oil-packed anchovy fillets, rinsed, patted dry, and minced
1 garlic clove, minced

Combine all ingredients in a bowl, and toss gently until blended. Store in an airtight container in the refrigerator up to 1 week. Serve at room temperature. **Yield: 1¾ cups.**

Use a computer to generate gift tags with serving suggestions included. ▶

Wrap Stars

Share the gift of creativity when you adorn presents with tags you've crafted yourself. Then use up those little scraps of wrapping paper by accenting party invitation envelopes with an extra burst of holiday charm.

▲ Anything Goes

Making gift tags is a great activity for kids. Gather a variety of plain tags, papers, and trimmings—and watch the fun begin! The tags pictured on these pages display a mix of materials to spark the imagination. Don't forget to search the toolbox for unusual embellishments, such as metal rings, bits of twine, and wire.

For a unique gift tag, cut a Christmas tree or snowman from a Fun Foam sheet, and glue the shape to a square of paper. Punch a hole in the tag, and tie it to a package with pretty ribbon (left).

◀ Matched Set

For party invitations, line the inside of each envelope with complementary gift wrap, and glue it in place. Finish the edges with a border of tiny rickrack. Embellish the envelope with a matching sticker or scrapbook cutout.

Giving Green

Months after the Christmas tree comes down, gifts of fresh plants continue to flourish.

Ambrosial Additions

For an extrasensory experience, give fragrant plants such as rosemary, lavender, and paperwhites that please through both sight and scent. Enhance the presentation by adding decorative elements—try scented pinecones, long twigs, faux berries, and ribbons—to the containers.

◀ Mug Shot

These gifts come together in no time by layering potting soil, paperwhite bulbs, and glass pebbles in coffee mugs. To create personalized gifts, search secondhand stores for inexpensive, one-of-a-kind mugs. Or for quick coordinated party favors, choose styles and colors that suit the theme of your party. The gifts keep giving because guests can use the mugs again and again.

▼ Grab Bag

For charming guest favors at casual gatherings, pick up a few pots of herbs while you're shopping for last-minute Christmas dinner items. (Fresh herbs are convenient because most grocers stock them year-round.) Reuse paper grocery bags to wrap the functional pots. Embellish the bags with ribbons, cards, or Christmas candies you have on hand to bring these gifts to life in less than five minutes.

Where to Find It

Source information is current at the time of publication; however, we cannot guarantee availability of items. If an item is not listed, its source is unknown.

Florist foam, picks, tape: Michaels, (800) 642-4235, www.michaels.com; www.smithersoasis.com; discount and crafts stores; local florist shops

• **page 12—metal stocking:** *Southern Living At HOME®;* www.southernlivingathome.com for ordering information

• **pages 14–15—pillar candles:** Pottery Barn; (888) 779-5176; www.potterybarn.com; **bud vases:** Anthropologie; (800) 309-2500; www.anthropologie.com

• **pages 16–17—containers:** *Southern Living At HOME®;* www.southernlivingathome.com for ordering information

• **pages 18–19—twig trees:** Oak Street Garden Shop; Birmingham, AL; (205) 870-7542; www.oakstreetgardenshop.com; **lacy ornaments:** Smith's Variety; Birmingham, AL; (205) 871-0841; **tree ornaments and star garland:** At Home; Homewood, AL; (205) 879-3510

• **pages 20–21—urns:** *Southern Living At HOME®;* www.southernlivingathome.com for ordering information

• **pages 22–23—stockings and snowflake votive containers:** Arcadia Home; (212) 366-1836; www.arcadiahomeinc.com; **lanterns, fire screen, urn with stand:** *Southern Living At HOME®;* www.southernlivingathome.com for ordering information; **letters on stands:** Anthropologie; (800) 309-2500; www.anthropologie.com; **silver sphere:** Pottery Barn; (888) 779-5176; www.potterybarn.com; **green pots:** Williams-Sonoma; (877) 812-6235; www.williams-sonoma.com; **red apple balls:** At Home; Homewood, AL; (205) 879-3510

• **pages 24–29—dinnerware:** R. Wood Studio Ceramics; Athens, GA; (888) 817-9663; www.rwoodstudio.com; **flatware:** Ballard Designs; (800) 536-7551; www.ballarddesigns.com; **napkins:** Anthropologie; (800) 309-2500;

www.anthropologie.com; **turquoise glasses:** Pier 1; (800) 245-4595; www.pier1.com; **red glasses:** Target; (800) 591-3869; www.target.com; **boot ornaments (with place cards), boot vases, tree ornaments, and boot stockings:** Seasons of Cannon Falls; (800) 377-3335; www.seasonsofcannonfalls.com; **cowboy boot stamp:** Hobby Lobby; (800) 888-0321, www.hobbylobby.com; **canteen lamp:** Woolrich; (877) 512-7305; www.woolrich.com; **tree ornaments and cowboy garland:** The Christmas Tree; Pelham, AL; (205) 988-8090; **metal mantel votives:** Red Rain; Homewood, AL; (205) 871-9282

• **page 30—cloches and stand:** Attic Antiques; Birmingham, AL; (205) 991-6887

• **page 31—tall plate stand and towel holder:** *Southern Living At HOME®;* www.southernlivingathome.com for ordering information; **cards:** Emily Parrish; www.toodleoodesigns.com; **ornaments:** Christmas & Co.; Birmingham, AL; (205) 823-6640; www.christmasandco.com

• **page 32—vintage Santas and ornaments:** At Home; Homewood, AL; (205) 879-3510; **urn:** *Southern Living At HOME®;* www.southernlivingathome.com for ordering information

• **page 33—wise men statues, candleholders, decorations:** Flora; Birmingham, AL; (205) 871-4004

• **pages 34–35—snowmen:** Christmas & Co.; Birmingham, AL; (205) 823-6640; www.christmasandco.com; **mirror:** *Southern Living At HOME®;* www.southernlivingathome.com for ordering information; **blue pots:** At Home; Homewood, AL; (205) 879-3510; **candy:** Elegant Gourmet; (425) 814-2500; www.elegantgourmet.com; **Santa hats and bag:** Pottery Barn; (888) 779-5176; www.potterybarn.com

• **pages 36–37— candy:** Elegant Gourmet; (425) 814-2500; www.elegantgourmet.com; **red linens:** Anthropologie; (800) 309-2500; www.anthropologie.com;

other linens: Table Matters; Birmingham, AL; (205) 879-0125; www.table-matters.com; **plates, picture-frame ornaments, snowmen ornaments:** Seasons of Cannon Falls; (800) 377-3335; www.seasonsofcannonfalls.com; **glasses:** S.F. Imports; (800) 969-1949; www.sfimports.com

• **page 38—candles:** Daedalus Candles; Birmingham, AL; (205) 871-1830; www.daedaluscandles.com; **cake stand:** Mariposa; Manchester, MA; (800) 788-1304; www.mariposa-gift.com; **red napkins:** Lamb's Ears, Ltd.; Birmingham, AL; (205) 969-3138; **plates:** T.J. Maxx; (800) 285-6299; www.tjmaxx.com

• **page 39—wheatgrass:** Tria Market; Homewood, AL; (205) 776-8923; www.triamarket.net; **container and mugs:** VIETRI; (866) 327-1279; www.vietri.com

• **pages 40–41—vases:** *Southern Living At HOME®;* www.southernlivingathome.com for ordering information; **tall vase:** Pottery Barn; (888) 779-5176; www.potterybarn.com

• **page 42—shot glasses:** At Home; Homewood, AL; (205) 879-3510

• **page 43—hourglass-shaped vase:** Cost Plus World Market; (877) 967-5362; www.worldmarket.com

• **page 45—hurricane vases:** *Southern Living At HOME®;* www.southernlivingathome.com for ordering information; **ornaments, garlands, tree, votive holders:** Christmas & Co.; Birmingham, AL; (205) 823-6640; www.christmasandco.com

• **pages 46–47—bowl and stand:** Attic Antiques; Birmingham, AL; (205) 991-6887

• **pages 48–49—plants:** Collier's Nursery; Birmingham, AL; (205) 822-3133; www.colliersnursery.com; **containers:** Attic Antiques, Birmingham, AL, (205) 991-6887; Maison de France Antiques, Leeds, AL, (205) 699-6330; Mulberry Heights Antiques, Birmingham, AL, (205) 870-1300

• **page 50—ornaments:** Christmas & Co., Birmingham, AL, (205) 823-6640, www.christmasandco.com; Lamb's Ears, Ltd., Birmingham, AL, (205) 969-3138; Pier 1, (800) 245-4595, www.pier1.com; Hobby Lobby, (800) 888-0321, www.hobbylobby.com

- **page 51**—reindeer and pedestal: Harmony Landing; Homewood, AL; (205) 871-0585; www.harmonylanding.com;
  candles: Daedalus Candles; Birmingham, AL; (205) 871-1830; www.daedaluscandles.com;
  snowballs: Flora; Birmingham, AL; (205) 871-4004
- **pages 52–53**—wagon: Little Hardware; Mountain Brook, AL; (205) 871-4616;
  ornaments and sock monkey Santa: Seasons of Cannon Falls; (800) 377-3335; www.seasonsofcannonfalls.com;
  alphabet letter: Anthropologie; (800) 309-2500; www.anthropologie.com;
  stocking: Pottery Barn Kids; (800) 993-4923; www.potterybarnkids.com
- **page 54**—white tree: At Home; Homewood, AL; (205) 879-3510;
  cookies: Edgar's Bakery; (205) 987-0790; www.edgarsbakery.com;
  table runner and ornaments: Pier 1; (800) 245-4595; www.pier1.com
- **page 56**—ornaments: The Christmas Tree; Pelham, AL; (205) 988-8090;
  star: Red Rain; Homewood, AL; (205) 871-9282;
  bucket and mug: Alice & Wonderland; Loxley, AL; (251) 964-4747;
  tags, milk jars, utensils: Seasons of Cannon Falls; (800) 377-3335; www.seasonsofcannonfalls.com;
  farm fresh sign: The Christmas Tree; Pelham, AL; (205) 988-8090
- **page 57**—assorted collectibles: The Christmas Tree, Pelham, AL, (205) 988-8090; Christmas & Co., Birmingham, AL, (205) 823-6640, www.christmasandco.com; At Home, Homewood, AL, (205) 879-3510; Christine's, Mountain Brook, AL, (205) 871-8297
- **page 60**—cake stand and mugs: Potluck Studios; Pittsfield, MA; (800) 559-7341; www.potluckstudios.com
- **page 61**—bowl and platter: Cook Store of Mountain Brook; Mountain Brook, AL; (205) 879-5277
- **page 63**—platter: Southern Fired Pottery & Glass; Edwards, MS; (601) 852-9109; www.southernfired.com
- **page 64**—cookware: Le Creuset; (877) 273-8738; www.lecreuset.com
- **page 68**—green linen: Nuko Creations, Inc.; West Long Branch, NJ; (732) 542-0200
- **page 71**—platter: Cook Store of Mountain Brook; Mountain Brook, AL; (205) 879-5277
- **page 74**—platter: Southern Fired Pottery & Glass; Edwards, MS; (601) 852-9109;

www.southernfired.com
- **page 77**—plate: VIETRI; (866) 327-1279; www.vietri.com
- **page 79**—cake stand: Juliska; Stamford, CT; (203) 316-0212; www.juliska.com
- **page 80**—plate: Seasons of Cannon Falls; (800) 377-3335; www.seasonsofcannonfalls.com
- **page 87**—cake stand: A'Mano; Mountain Brook, AL; (205) 871-9093
- **page 91**—snowman: Seasons of Cannon Falls; (800) 377-3335; www.seasonsofcannonfalls.com
- **pages 98–103**—mantel tins: *Southern Living At HOME®*; www.southernlivingathome.com for ordering information;
  transferware: Mulberry Heights Antiques; Birmingham, AL; (205) 870-1300;
  pumpkin candles: Pottery Barn; (888) 779-5176; www.potterybarn.com;
  centerpiece container: Collier's Nursery; Birmingham, AL; (205) 822-3133; www.colliersnursery.com;
  landscape design: Terrebonne Landscape Architectural Design; Birmingham, AL; (205) 323-4939;
  tablecloth: Anthropologie; (800) 309-2500; www.anthropologie.com;
  glasses and napkins: Swoozie's; (866) 796-6943; www.swoozies.com;
  demitasse cups: Bed, Bath & Beyond; (800) 462-3966; www.bedbathandbeyond.com
- **pages 104–107**—dinnerware, table runners, candleholders, pinecone candles, napkins: Pottery Barn; (888) 779-5176; www.potterybarn.com;
  glasses, chair star, chapel: Lamb's Ears, Ltd.; Birmingham, AL; (205) 969-3138;
  flatware: Madison Bay Company; East Berlin, PA; (717) 259-6886;
  twig trees: Davis Wholesale Florist; Birmingham, AL; (205) 595-2179
- **pages 108–111**—Accent Wardian Case, Tabletop Wardian Case: H. Potter; Coeur d'Alene, ID; (509) 921-1640; www.hpotter.com;
  votive holders and table runner: Table Matters; Birmingham, AL; (205) 879-0125; www.table-matters.com;
  glasses: Anthropologie; (800) 309-2500; www.anthropologie.com;
  tablecloth: Pottery Barn; (888) 779-5176; www.potterybarn.com;
  chairs: Mulberry Heights Antiques; Birmingham, AL; (205) 870-1300;
  mercury trees, plates, crystal rings: Barreveld International; (845) 265-6052;

www.barreveld.com;
  napkins: Nuko Creations, Inc.; West Long Branch, NJ; (732) 542-0200;
  stockings: Traces of Time; Anniston, AL; (256) 741-9500
- **pages 112–113**—dried lemon leaf wreaths, place mats, napkins: Table Matters; Birmingham, AL; (205) 879-0125; www.table-matters.com;
  glasses: Lamb's Ears, Ltd.; Birmingham, AL; (205) 969-3138;
  brown chargers: Pottery Barn; (888) 779-5176; www.potterybarn.com
- **page 117**—silver and bronze setting: Pier 1; (800) 245-4595; www.pier1.com
- **pages 118–119**—plates: Mariposa; (800) 788-1304; www.mariposa-gift.com;
  wineglasses: Williams-Sonoma; (877) 812-6235; www.williams-sonoma.com
- **page 126**—bowl: Mariposa; (800) 788-1304; www.mariposa-gift.com
- **pages 130–134**—metal cake stand and mugs: Gracious Goods; Overland Park, KS; (866) 238-6448;
  other mugs: A'Mano; Mountain Brook, AL; (205) 871-9093;
  chargers: *Southern Living At HOME®*; www.southernlivingathome.com for ordering information;
  pottery: Cook Store of Mountain Brook; Mountain Brook, AL; (205) 879-5277;
  salad bowl: Southern Fired Pottery & Glass; Edwards, MS; (601) 852-9109; www.southernfired.com
- **page 136**—glasses: Pier 1; (800) 245-4595; www.pier1.com
- **page 140**—trays: *Southern Living At HOME®*; www.southernlivingathome.com for ordering information;
  plates: Cook Store of Mountain Brook; Mountain Brook, AL; (205) 879-5277
- **pages 146–147**—white pedestal bowls: *Southern Living At HOME®*; www.southernlivingathome.com for ordering information
- **page 152**—bowls: Pottery Barn; (888) 779-5176; www.potterybarn.com
- **page 157**—smoked sea salt: Halen Môn smoked sea salt; (800) 353-7258; www.saltworks.us
- **page 159**—snowmen mugs: Williams-Sonoma; (877) 812-6235; www.williams-sonoma.com
- **pages 164–165**—jars: Cost Plus World Market; (877) 967-5362; www.worldmarket.com

Recipe Index

General Index

Contributors

Editorial Contributors

Margaret Agnew
Lorrie Hulston Corvin
Georgia Downard
Caroline Grant
Alyson Haynes

Susan Huff
Beth Jordan
Ana Kelly
Jackie Mills

Thanks to the following homeowners

Kelley and Thomas Alford
Betsy and David Bell
Catherine and Doug Coltharp
David Coyne
Donna and Bill Davis
Margaret and Will Dickey
Patsy and Alan Dreher
Sharon and Emris Graham
Beth and James Jordan
Amy and Michael Murphree

Nancy and Mark Peeples
Martha Robinson
Kathy and Tommy Sanders
Susie and Mike Schor
Tyler Sims
Frances and Robert Stanford
Laura and Jeff Taylor
Jan and Kyle Ware
Sandra and Ben Zarzaur

Thanks to these Birmingham businesses and organizations

A'Mano
Anthropologie
Bromberg's
Christine's
Christmas & Co. / FlowerBuds, Inc.
The Christmas Tree
Davis Wholesale Flowers
Flora
Lamb's Ears, Ltd.
Little Hardware

Mulberry Heights
Oak Street Garden Shop
Pottery Barn
Rosegate
Smith's Variety
Swoozie's
Table Matters
Terrebonne Landscape Architectural Design
Tricia's Treasures

holiday planner

Make organizing easy with this special section that offers planning calendars, decorating tips, handy cooking references, and lots of space for making lists.

November

Sunday	Monday	Tuesday	Wednesday
4	5	6	7
11	12	13	14
18	19	20	21
25	26	27	28

2007

Thursday	Friday	Saturday
1	2	3
8	9	10
15	16	17
Thanksgiving 22	23	24
29	30	

get set for the season

Checking off these items in November means more free time in December!

☐ Plan the Thanksgiving menu early in the month, and start a grocery list for the big feast.
☐ Gather leaves, branches, and dried materials for harvest decorating. Use potted mums, pansies, and small pumpkins to augment the natural materials.
☐ Check table linens to see what needs to be replaced or cleaned.
☐ Give the house a thorough cleaning so it can be ready for entertaining at a moment's notice.
☐ Prepare holiday make-ahead dishes.
☐ Stock up on ingredients for quick snacks to serve to unexpected guests.
☐ Purchase Christmas cards, and get them ready to mail.
☐ Buy gift-wrapping materials, including boxes and bags, tags, ribbons, and tape.

things to do

December

Sunday	Monday	Tuesday	Wednesday
2	3	4	5
9	10	11	12
16	17	18	19
23 / 30	24 Christmas Eve / New Year's Eve 31	Christmas 25	26

2007

Thursday	Friday	Saturday
		1
6	7	8
13	14	15
20	21	22
27	28	29

holiday-ready pantry

Be prepared for seasonal cooking and baking by stocking up on these items.

☐ Assorted coffees, teas, hot chocolate, and eggnog

☐ Wine, beer, and soft drinks

☐ White, brown, and powdered sugars

☐ Ground allspice, cinnamon, cloves, ginger, and nutmeg

☐ Baking soda and baking powder

☐ Seasonal fresh herbs

☐ Baking chocolate

☐ Semisweet chocolate morsels

☐ Assorted nuts

☐ Flaked coconut

☐ Sweetened condensed milk and evaporated milk

☐ Whipping cream

☐ Jams, jellies, and preserves

☐ Raisins, cranberries, and other fresh or dried fruits

☐ Canned pumpkin

☐ Frozen/refrigerated bread dough, biscuits, and croissants

things to do

ribbon trimmings

Use ribbon to transform everyday objects into cheery holiday accents. Get started with these suggestions.

• **Use ribbon as a garland.** Drape lengths of ribbon across windows, atop doorways, and along mantels. Secure the ribbon swags with an adhesive that won't harm painted finishes, such as painter's tape or mounting putty.

• **Give yourself a complement.** Coordinate decorations with your room's color scheme by tying ribbons in complementary hues around vases or lamps. Tie ribbons around clusters of boxwood or cedar; wire the beribboned swags to the fireplace tool stand, or use them to adorn mirrors or paintings.

• **Treat your cabinet doors like presents.** Place lengths of ribbon from the top to the bottom of a cabinet door and then repeat from side to side. Tie a big bow at the intersection of the ribbons.

• **Create a centerpiece.** Make a simple cake stand the center of attention by tying a bow around the pedestal. Use double-faced satin ribbon for a soft, luxurious bow. Display your favorite holiday cake on the stand, or group several pillar candles on it for a decoration that will last all season.

• **Fancy up the sideboard.** Add an interesting focal point to a sideboard or buffet by placing brightly colored napkins tied with pretty ribbons in a vase.

• **Take a shortcut.** Use leftover scraps of ribbon to dress up clear jar candles to give as hostess gifts or party favors. Wrap a length of grosgrain ribbon around the center of each jar; glue a holiday charm to the center of the ribbon to add a finishing touch.

• **Make a memory.** With a fine-tip permanent marker, write your name and the year on a narrow piece of ribbon; then attach the ribbon as a hanger on a special ornament to give as a gift.

Decorating To-Do List

Having all your materials assembled beforehand makes decorating your home more fun—and stress free.

Gather materials

from the yard ....

from around the house ....
....

from the store ....
....

other ....

Add holiday decorations

to the table ....
....

to the door ....
....

to the mantel ....
....

to the staircase ....
....

other ....
....

perfect timing
Follow these easy guidelines to organize your menu and recipes so that every dish is hot and ready on time.

Turkey and family-favorite sides are the crowning glory of many holiday feasts. However, if all of your dishes have to go in the oven—and at different temperatures and times—you may have trouble juggling. Here are ways for you to modify your menu so that all your dishes come out together.

Start with the Turkey
• It can take 2 to 3 days to thaw a frozen turkey. So buy it ahead of time while the selection is still plentiful, and plan when and how you'll thaw it. Find defrosting charts attached to the turkey, or visit www.butterball.com.

• After the turkey thaws, stick your hand into the cavity and pull out the neck and giblets. They're usually wrapped in paper. If you forget this step and find these after you've finished cooking, your turkey is still safe to eat.

• Once you've removed the turkey from the oven, cover it loosely with foil to allow the bird to rest (approximately 15 to 20 minutes). The juices will absorb back into the turkey, making it easy to carve. This resting time allows for prime oven time for casseroles or desserts.

In the Oven
• After the turkey's done, decide whether you can fit one or two baking dishes into your oven and position the racks accordingly. For older ovens, allow extra time if baking more than one item; you may also need to rotate the dishes halfway through the bake time for even baking and browning. The technology for newer ovens allows them a standard baking time, regardless of how many dishes are placed in the oven.

• Multiple items may be baked at the same time if they require the same baking temperature. When you're creating your menu, keep an eye on temperatures and bake times to make coordination easy.

Oven Alternatives
• If your oven can't accommodate everything on your menu, consider replacing some recipes with ones that rely on a slow cooker, microwave, or cooktop. Steam vegetables or cook potatoes in the microwave; or sauté fresh vegetables on the cooktop. You can also microwave hard squashes, such as acorns and butternuts. Make casseroles ahead of time in microwave-safe dishes (make sure they fit in your microwave), and reheat them just prior to serving.

• When using the slow cooker, set it on a cutting board to protect your countertop from heat fluctuations that might cause it to crack. Make cleanup easy with a slow-cooker liner (it's like a plastic bag that fits inside your slow cooker), available at the supermarket. Just lift out the bag from the slow cooker after the food is removed, and toss it.

About Desserts
• When it comes to preparing dessert for a holiday meal, consider offering selections that can be made ahead of time, such as cakes, some pies, and chilled desserts. Other dessert items, such as cobblers and bread puddings, can go into the oven just before you sit down to eat and come out hot when you finish the meal.

The Roasting Pan

A turkey is best cooked on a rack in a shallow roasting pan. If your roasting pan is missing the rack, line the bottom with 1½" of roughly chopped fruits and vegetables (such as onions, celery, carrots, and apples). These elevate the bird off the pan and add wonderful flavor. Plus, the rich pan drippings make a delicious gravy. Keep these things in mind when selecting a roasting pan:

• For ease of cleanup, choose a large disposable aluminum foil pan, available at the supermarket. Place it on a baking sheet for support.

• Avoid deep Dutch ovens with high sides (more than 4 inches), and don't use a lid; you'll get a steamed turkey rather than a browned roasted one.

• A good roasting pan costs from $45 to $60. We like a stainless exterior with a dark nonstick interior and sturdy handles.

---

party planner

Use this chart to coordinate menu items for your holiday celebration, as well as a reminder of who's bringing what.

guests	what they're bringing	serving pieces needed
	☐appetizer ☐beverage ☐bread ☐main dish ☐side dish ☐dessert	
	☐appetizer ☐beverage ☐bread ☐main dish ☐side dish ☐dessert	
	☐appetizer ☐beverage ☐bread ☐main dish ☐side dish ☐dessert	
	☐appetizer ☐beverage ☐bread ☐main dish ☐side dish ☐dessert	
	☐appetizer ☐beverage ☐bread ☐main dish ☐side dish ☐dessert	
	☐appetizer ☐beverage ☐bread ☐main dish ☐side dish ☐dessert	
	☐appetizer ☐beverage ☐bread ☐main dish ☐side dish ☐dessert	
	☐appetizer ☐beverage ☐bread ☐main dish ☐side dish ☐dessert	
	☐appetizer ☐beverage ☐bread ☐main dish ☐side dish ☐dessert	
	☐appetizer ☐beverage ☐bread ☐main dish ☐side dish ☐dessert	
	☐appetizer ☐beverage ☐bread ☐main dish ☐side dish ☐dessert	
	☐appetizer ☐beverage ☐bread ☐main dish ☐side dish ☐dessert	
	☐appetizer ☐beverage ☐bread ☐main dish ☐side dish ☐dessert	
	☐appetizer ☐beverage ☐bread ☐main dish ☐side dish ☐dessert	
	☐appetizer ☐beverage ☐bread ☐main dish ☐side dish ☐dessert	
	☐appetizer ☐beverage ☐bread ☐main dish ☐side dish ☐dessert	
	☐appetizer ☐beverage ☐bread ☐main dish ☐side dish ☐dessert	
	☐appetizer ☐beverage ☐bread ☐main dish ☐side dish ☐dessert	

Party Guest List

Pantry List

Party To-Do List

Christmas dinner planner

Fill in the charts on these pages to help you organize the grand Christmas feast. Then use them as a good reference when next December rolls around.

Menu Ideas

....
....
....
....
....
....
....
....
....

Dinner To-Do List

....
....
....
....
....
....
....
....
....
....

Christmas Dinner Guest List

....

....

....

....

....

....

....

....

....

....

....

Microwave Melting Times

Place a copy of this timetable where you can use it as a handy reference. Be sure to use microwave-safe containers, and cover them to avoid splatters. Start with the shortest time listed, and then add time as needed.

Melting butter:
Place in a microwave-safe glass measuring cup; microwave at HIGH until melted, stirring after the shortest time. For ½ cup or larger, cut sticks of butter in half.

1 to 2 tablespoons	35 to 40 seconds
¼ to ½ cup	40 to 45 seconds
¾ cup	40 to 50 seconds
1 cup	50 to 60 seconds

Melting chocolate morsels:
Place in a microwave-safe glass measuring cup; microwave at HIGH until melted, stirring after 30 seconds.

¼ to 1 cup	50 to 60 seconds

Melting chocolate baking squares:
Place in a microwave-safe glass measuring cup; microwave at HIGH until melted, stirring every 30 seconds.

1-ounce baking square	30 to 40 seconds
2-ounce baking square	60 to 90 seconds

Clip & Keep Holiday Hotlines

These toll-free telephone numbers and Web sites can provide you with quick answers to last-minute questions about roasting turkeys, baking, and food-safety issues.

- USDA Meat & Poultry Hotline: 1-800-535-4555
- FDA Center for Food Safety: 1-888-723-3366
- Butterball Turkey Talk Line: 1-800-288-8372 or www.butterball.com
- The Reynolds Kitchen Tips Line: 1-800-745-4000 or www.reynoldskitchens.com
- Fleischmann's Yeast: 1-800-777-4959 or www.fleischmanns.com
- Betty Crocker (General Mills): 1-888-275-2388 or www.bettycrocker.com
- Nestlé Baking: 1-800-637-8537 or www.verybestbaking.com
- Ocean Spray: 1-800-662-3263 or www.oceanspray.com

gifts and greetings

Write your gift and Christmas card lists here, and fill in the size charts for a gift-buying reference you'll consult year-round.

Gift List and Size Charts

name /sizes	gift purchased/made	sent/delivered

name ....

jeans_____ shirt_____ sweater_____ jacket_____ shoes_____ belt_____

blouse_____ skirt_____ slacks_____ dress_____ suit_____ coat_____

pajamas_____ robe_____ hat_____ gloves_____ ring_____

name ....

jeans_____ shirt_____ sweater_____ jacket_____ shoes_____ belt_____

blouse_____ skirt_____ slacks_____ dress_____ suit_____ coat_____

pajamas_____ robe_____ hat_____ gloves_____ ring_____

name ....

jeans_____ shirt_____ sweater_____ jacket_____ shoes_____ belt_____

blouse_____ skirt_____ slacks_____ dress_____ suit_____ coat_____

pajamas_____ robe_____ hat_____ gloves_____ ring_____

name ....

jeans_____ shirt_____ sweater_____ jacket_____ shoes_____ belt_____

blouse_____ skirt_____ slacks_____ dress_____ suit_____ coat_____

pajamas_____ robe_____ hat_____ gloves_____ ring_____

name ....

jeans_____ shirt_____ sweater_____ jacket_____ shoes_____ belt_____

blouse_____ skirt_____ slacks_____ dress_____ suit_____ coat_____

pajamas_____ robe_____ hat_____ gloves_____ ring_____

name ....

jeans_____ shirt_____ sweater_____ jacket_____ shoes_____ belt_____

blouse_____ skirt_____ slacks_____ dress_____ suit_____ coat_____

pajamas_____ robe_____ hat_____ gloves_____ ring_____

name ....

jeans_____ shirt_____ sweater_____ jacket_____ shoes_____ belt_____

blouse_____ skirt_____ slacks_____ dress_____ suit_____ coat_____

pajamas_____ robe_____ hat_____ gloves_____ ring_____

188

Christmas Card List

name	address	sent/delivered

holiday memories

Keep the best parts of seasonal celebrations fresh by jotting down highlights on these pages.

Treasured Traditions

Write your family's favorite holiday traditions on these lines.

....
....
....
....
....
....
....
....
....
....

Special Holiday Activities

List events you attended this year, and also note those you want to check out for next year.

....
....
....
....
....

Holiday Visits and Visitors

Record special visitors, houseguests, and friends and family news updates on these lines.

....
....
....
....
....
....
....
....
....
....
....
....
....
....
....
....
....
....
....
....
....
....
....
....
....
....

This Year's Favorite Recipes

Appetizers and Beverages ....
....
....
....

Entrées ....
....
....

Sides and Salads ....
....
....

Cookies and Candies..
....
....

Desserts..
....
....
....

looking ahead

Holiday Wrap-up

Make a list of thank-you notes to be sent for gifts and holiday hospitality.

name	gift and/or event	note sent
		☐
		☐
		☐
		☐
		☐
		☐
		☐
		☐
		☐
		☐
		☐
		☐
		☐

Notes for Next Year

Start planning for the 2008 holiday season while memories of Christmas 2007 are still fresh.